BLUEPRINT FOR TEACHING

JOHN T. SISEMORE

BROADMAN PRESS
Nashville, Tennessee

DEWEY DECIMAL CLASSIFICATION: 268.6
Library of Congress catalog card number: 64–12413
Printed in the United States of America

Contents

1

To Plan or Not to Plan

Teaching is a venture in faith—faith in God, faith in his Word, and faith in the miracle of teaching itself. Yet, faith alone will not produce effective learning. To his faith the teacher must add an understanding of teaching, a knowledge of the learning process, and skill in planning and directing the class session.

As far as the classroom experience is concerned, the basic task of the teacher is to create and control the learning environment while, at the same time, stimulating and guiding the learners in their exploration of truth.

Teaching, then, is more than relating Bible stories, facts, and events. It is more than moralizing and exhorting learners to "live better"; it is also more than asking questions, giving lectures, or stimulating a discussion. Teaching is much more than the skilful employment of current methods, devices, and techniques in instruction.

Teaching is a difficult and an exacting art which requires a well-prepared, creative, and alert teacher. It requires a teacher who can organize learning activities and keep them moving toward definite outcomes. Effective teaching is emphatically not a matter of chance and circumstance. Neither is it the strict observance of the rules of teaching or the laws of learning. Teaching is the outcome and consequence of planning. It is guiding learners in activities that have meaning and purpose for them. Does it not follow then that fruitful Bible teaching calls for more than a dedicated Christian worker? Does it not require more than a working knowledge of the Bible? Does it not demand more than just a mere familiarity with current methodology and procedures?

Successful teaching—teaching that changes lives and promotes growth toward Christian maturity—waits on the skilful planning, organizing, and timing of appropriate learning experiences. In short, the Christian teacher must add intelligent planning to spirituality.

James L. Mursell writes:

> Some progressive educators are fond of insisting that a teacher should never plan "in advance of the situation." Presumably what they are attacking is rigid planning, narrow planning, trial-and-error planning. . . . For not to plan at all is even more disastrous and destructive than to plan rigidly.[1]

To be sure, planning is involved in all teaching no matter how haphazard or illogical it may be. However, the quality of the planning largely determines the quality of the teaching and, consequently, the quality of the learning.

The Bible Magnifies Planning

Although the Bible is the divinely inspired Word of God, its effectiveness can be either helped or hindered by human hands. It is undoubtably true that no matter how poorly it is taught, the Bible will accomplish some good. On the other hand, the teacher who has thoroughly planned his teaching procedure becomes a better channel by which the Word of God may work more fruitfully.

How then does the Bible magnify planning?

By requiring planned teaching.—The *Amplified New Testament* translates 2 Timothy 2:15 as follows:

---

[1] *Successful Teaching* (New York: McGraw-Hill Book Co., 1954), p. 306.

Study and be eager and do your utmost to present yourself to God approved (tested by trial), a workman who has no cause to be ashamed, correctly analyzing and accurately dividing—rightly handling and skilfully teaching—the Word of Truth.

Notice how each descriptive phrase about teaching waits upon and depends upon careful planning—"rightly handling, correctly analyzing." Even the injunction to study is based on the importance of the teacher's finding God's approval by not bringing shame upon himself for his lack of planning and preparation. Assuredly, God can and does use a teacher who is ignorant. But will he use one who is indolent?

By commending orderly teaching.—Phillips translates 2 Timothy 3:16 as follows: "All scripture is inspired by God and is useful for teaching the faith and correcting error, for resetting the direction of a man's life and training him in good living."

In this passage Paul emphasizes the use of the Bible in an orderly, planned approach to teaching. At least four specific areas of teaching are mentioned: (1) communication of the divine revelation—"teaching the faith"; (2) conviction of personal sin—"correcting error"; (3) direction of the moral life—"resetting the direction of a man's life"; and (4) instruction in holy living—"training him in good living."

Each of these areas is specific, logical, and systematic. Such teaching cannot be done effectively without study and planning. Also in 2 Timothy 2:2, Paul instructs Timothy to teach systematically those who are qualified to carry on the teaching ministry in a competent manner.

By emphasizing specific purposes in teaching.—The practical, purposeful teaching of the Scriptures held an important place in the life of the Hebrew people. To them, the teaching of the Word of God was not necessarily an end in itself. It was a means of creating a godly nation. In other words, teaching was purposeful.

Moses charged Israel to "gather the people together, men, and women, and children, and thy stranger that is within thy gates, that they may hear, and that they may learn, and fear the Lord your God, and observe to do all the words of this law" (Deut. 31:12). Throughout the Bible, the references to teaching indicate a definite purpose toward which teaching is to be directed.

The Holy Spirit Honors Planning

Unfortunately, some teachers seem to misunderstand the role of the Holy Spirit in teaching, for they do little or no advance planning. They simply hope, and sometimes pray, that the Lord will guide them. They rely on the inspiration of the moment as they extemporize a "lesson." On the other hand, it appears that some teachers overlook, or even ignore, the ministry of the Holy Spirit, for they study, plan, and teach without relying on the help of the Spirit.

Actually, the teacher and the Holy Spirit are partners in teaching, each one being mutually dependent on the other. The teacher can work without the help of the Holy Spirit, but his efforts are fruitless. The Holy Spirit can work without the teacher, but his work is greatly facilitated when the teacher takes the time and trouble to plan.

By guiding the teacher in his planning.—The Holy Spirit is not bound by limitations of time and space. His assistance is not confined to the actual moment of need. He can and does work in advance of every situation in which the teacher finds himself. Furthermore, the Spirit apparently helps the teacher more who plans well—both in the planning stage and at the time of teaching.

As the teacher prayerfully studies and plans for effective teaching, he has scriptural assurance that he may count on the help and guidance of the Holy Spirit. "Howbeit when he, the Spirit of truth, is come, he will *guide* you into all truth" (John 16:13). "Now we have received, not the spirit of the world, but the spirit which is of God; that we might know the things that are freely given to us of God" (1 Cor. 2:12).

By reinforcing the prepared teacher.—The Holy Spirit works through the teacher's God-given intelligence, fortifying and reinforcing him in his efforts. The teacher who has planned carefully is encouraged by Christ's promise, "But the Comforter, which is the Holy Ghost, whom the Father will send in my name, he shall teach you all things, and bring all things to your remembrance" (John 14:26).

Obviously, the teacher who gives no time or thought to his teaching cannot count on the Lord to "fill his mouth." The Holy Spirit does not work in a vacuum but through the laws of teaching and learning which God himself has provided.

Planning Rightly Relates Teaching to Learning

The vital relationship between teaching and learning has been grossly misunderstood. Far too long teachers have paid more attention to the transmission of facts than to the translation of truth by the learners. Proper planning will greatly help in overcoming the false notion that teaching is spraying pupils with truth and that learning is absorbing the spray.

By enlarging the concept of learning.—As the teacher develops skill in planning his teaching procedure, he gradually becomes aware of the fact that his concept of teaching is too limited. He discovers that learning is much more than knowledge, for knowledge simply is one's accumulated store of information. He realizes that learning is *changing*. Learning is *growing*. Learning is *becoming*.

Teaching is a process; learning is the product. Teaching is a procedure; learning is an outcome. Teaching is a means; learning is the end.

The only teaching that *is* teaching is that which produces desirable changes in the life of the learner. And the only learning that changes conduct significantly is the learning that is self-discovered and self-appropriated.

By clarifying the role of the teacher.—Skilful planning causes the teacher to analyze his role in the teaching-learning process. What must he do if his members are to learn well and if he is to achieve lasting, usable, and meaningful results?

If learning is growing, then the teacher must include in his planning the arrangement of conditions that produce growth. He must organize learning activities and plan to guide his members in their learning experiences. He must plan the learning activities, create the learning climate, stimulate the search for truth, guide the learning "applications," and get the learning into life. It follows then that the teacher can accomplish these complex and exacting objectives only through careful planning and expert strategy.

By re-evaluating the focus of teaching.—The teacher who plans thoughtfully must inevitably face the problem of focus in teaching. He must determine whether the Bible, the pupil, or the teacher shall be the focal point.

Essentially, the Bible is the textbook of the Sunday school, even though Bible truth is organized into units and lesson helps are provided. However, the Bible—divinely inspired as it is— is impersonal until it becomes related to human motives and needs. The teacher must, therefore, focus upon the spiritual needs of the members. He must use the Bible as the authority and the source of learning. He must consider himself the integrating factor in the entire teaching-learning procedure.

This concept brings the Bible, the learner, and the teacher into a balanced relationship. As a result, teaching is "reality-centered." This means that the "center of teaching" does not rest entirely or even largely on either the Bible, the learner, or the teacher. Rather, there is a realistic balance on all three. The Bible is the *organizational* center around which the content and context of the curriculum are developed. The learner is the *directional* center around which the learning experiences and activities are developed. The teacher is the *inspirational* center from which the stimulation and challenge to learn emerge.

Planning Introduces the Long Look in Teaching

Planning adds a continuing perspective to teaching that is noticeably absent when preparation is haphazard or incomplete. Without the long look which long-range planning produces, teaching is little more than a dull routine of getting off a lesson of the S.O.S. (same old stuff) variety, finding something to say on Sunday or just filibustering for the Lord!

Planning introduces the long look into teaching in at least three ways.

By appraising the spiritual status of the learner.—Each class member is a unique individual in every way. Physically, socially, mentally, emotionally, and spiritually each one differs from the others. Although there are many similarities among the members, the differences are far more important to the teacher, for the growth of each member is paramount.

If teaching is directed toward helping each learner approach "unto a perfect [spiritually mature] man, unto the measure of the stature of the fulness of Christ" (Eph. 4:13), and it certainly is, then the teacher must be aware of the spiritual condition of his members at all times.

A regular part of the teacher's planning is a thorough appraisal of the spiritual needs of the class members, both collectively and individually. He evaluates his impressions in the light of his personal observations, the records of the class, and the response of the various members.

As the teacher appraises the spiritual condition of his members, he will become aware of the fact that other teachers and former experiences have helped lay the spiritual foundations of his members. The long look, which includes looking back and understanding these influences, helps the teacher by enabling him to build on them or alter them as the need may arise.

By focusing on the lifelong objectives of teaching.—The long look includes, not only the appraisal of the present and an appreciation of the past, but a goal for the future as well. These goals are generally looked upon as lifelong objectives. They have been stated in several ways with varying degrees of detail. The following brief statements are an adaptation of "The Objectives of Christian Teaching and Training"[2] of the Baptist Sunday School Board of the Southern Baptist Convention appearing in *The Curriculum Guide, 1962–63.*

---

[2] Clifton J. Allen and W. L. Howse (eds.) *The Curriculum Guide, 1962–63* (Nashville: Convention Press, 1962), p. 15.

1. Lead each unsaved person to a genuine experience of the forgiving and saving grace of God through Jesus Christ.

2. Guide each Christian into intelligent, active, and devoted membership in a New Testament church.

3. Help each Christian to make worship a vital and constant part of his expanding experience.

4. Help each Christian to grow toward mature Christian knowledge, understanding, and conviction.

5. Assist each Christian in developing such attitudes and appreciations that he will have a Christian approach to all of life.

6. Guide each Christian in developing habits and skills which promote spiritual growth and in applying Christian standards of conduct in every area of life.

7. Lead each Christian to invest his talents and skills in Christian service.

By forecasting the desired contributions of each unit and lesson.—The basic consideration in long-range planning is to determine the desired learning outcomes of each unit and lesson. Each outcome should grow out of, and be related to, the lifelong objectives. It should make a permanent contribution to cumulative growth toward these objectives. The teacher, to take the long look, should decide what knowledge and understanding, what attitudes and appreciations, what abilities and skills, what individual and class conduct should be sought in each lesson.

These projected learning outcomes are not general, indefinite results for some hypothetical class. Rather, they are specific outcomes for individual members in the teacher's own particular class. In other words, the teacher does not forecast "wholesale" learning but "retail" learning.

It should be obvious that long-range planning has a preliminary quality. The interests, purposes, and unfolding needs of the members will require alteration, addition, and even omission of some parts of the plan. However, the groundwork must be laid, and the learning possibilities must be carefully thought through. The teacher should always keep in mind that what the members are to be, they are now becoming.

Planning Improves the Teacher's Skill

Any teacher who is worthy of the name realizes that he never reaches a state of efficiency that eliminates the possibility of improvement. Even the best teachers are subject to refinements of skill, technique, and personal improvement. Unquestionably, the skilful teacher is a growing teacher, and the growing teacher is a planning teacher.

Just how does planning help the teacher become more skilful and effective in his art?

By keeping the teacher from becoming satisfied.—Probably the most important ingredient in skilful teaching is a continuing dissatisfaction with one's present ability in teaching. Coupled with this basic attitude, there must be an unrelenting and enthusiastic effort to reach a higher plane of effectiveness. However, without careful, diligent planning at every stage of preparation and without thoughtful, objective evaluation of one's plan, a teacher may easily drift into deadly routines and practices. Planning is, therefore, the basic protection against monotony, the best motivation toward improvement, and the best guarantee against self-satisfaction.

By establishing a proper sense of direction.—Too many teachers are like the purported general who got on his horse and rode off in all directions at the same time! Too often the major goal of the teacher seems to be merely to have enough material to last for the thirty-minute session or to be able "to cover the lesson."

Planning helps the teacher relate single lessons to units and units to lifelong objectives. Planning helps the teacher relate lessons to pupil needs and interests. Planning helps the teacher point his members in the direction of Christ "that the man of God may be perfect, thoroughly furnished unto all good works" (2 Tim. 3:17). Planning helps the teacher direct his full effort toward the upbuilding of those taught in the perfecting of godly character and Christian fruitfulness.

By utilizing the best methods of learning.—It has been often said that "it makes little difference how one likes to teach, if the members do not learn in that particular way."

Teaching techniques and learning methods are simply tools; they are a means to a teaching end. Planning is, therefore, the secret of matching the truth to be taught with a method by which the truth can be learned. Of course, "teaching cannot be reduced to a standard foolproof routine," but planning can certainly simplify the process.

Methods are also devices for inducing members to self-activity. Therefore, methods need to be suited to the individual learner as well as to the kind of material to be taught. This procedure also requires diligent and prayerful planning, for the teacher is essentially an organizer of learning activities.

By simplifying the handling of unpredicted influences.—The most thoughtful and expert teachers will inevitably face experiences and influences in the classroom that are totally unexpected or unanticipated. These influences must be dealt with effectively. Is it not apparent that the teacher who honestly tries to anticipate every happening in the classroom is in a much better position to cope with the unexpected than the teacher who prefers to "play it by ear"?

By making learning meaningful to the members.—Every avenue of planning must eventually converge at the point of making learning meaningful to the members. Actually, the problem of helping members to learn is a matter of teaching them to think, and teaching learners to think is a problem of making learning experiences meaningful to them. Such experiences are centered in keeping teaching and learning activities in the areas of interest, need, and challenge for every member.

So, to plan or not to plan—that is the question. But be aware of the fact that planning makes good teaching, and planning makes good teachers!

2
Blueprint for Teaching

Learning is a volitional matter. One learns only as he desires to learn. Learning, therefore, can never be forced, stereotyped, or circumscribed. There must be freedom in learning—freedom of choice, freedom of will, and freedom of privilege.

On the other hand, the freedom to learn requires organization, limitations, and even a certain structuring. Otherwise, chaos would result; there would be no opportunity for learning and little desire to learn. Actually, it is the flexibility within limits that heightens the will to learn and produces the factors that make for good learning.

But what are the limits and how are they determined? These limits are the outgrowth of the teacher's preplanning and the consequent modifications made by the learners.

Planning, when properly understood, amounts to living through the class session in advance. It is an anticipation of all that will transpire. As the teacher draws on his experience, pupil knowledge, and teaching proficiency, a workable plan of procedure gradually takes shape. This kind of "preliving" a lesson is real planning.

Planning, when it is effective, must eventually culminate in a written plan of procedure for the class session. The resulting document is a teaching plan. It is a blueprint for teaching, and the teacher's success depends to a large degree on his ability to create such a workable, flexible guide sheet.

What Is a Teaching Plan?

This question is not an easy one to answer. The field has not been thoroughly explored, especially in the realm of Christian teaching. The teacher's basic philosophy of teaching, which he may not even realize he possesses, his personal temperament, and background of experience will all influence his concept of the teaching plan.

Some negative considerations are enlightening.—Clarity of thought and insight are frequently aided by first clearing away the negative aspects of a question.

1. A teaching plan is not a homiletical outline of the Scripture passage. The ability to construct a homiletical outline is essential to good preaching, and it is an art in itself. However, the ability to create a good homiletical message is not a prerequisite to skilful teaching. In fact, this kind of preparation when looked upon as a teaching plan can be a handicap to effective teaching. On the other hand, the ability to reduce the Scripture truth to a simple outline is a distinct advantage to the teacher. But even this type of outline does not constitute a teaching plan.

2. A teaching plan is not a formal speech. Although there is valuable discipline in learning to create a formal message, the customary introduction, development, and conclusion used in such messages are far too stereotyped for teaching. Only the confirmed, unbending lecturer could accept this procedure as a teaching plan.

3. A teaching plan is not merely a chronological arrangement of events. A step-by-step arrangement of events is probably the easiest and most natural method of organizing any material. Likely, this plan is the least effective even when the Bible material is chronologically organized. The fault of this method is apparent. It focuses attention on the material, content, and information to be taught rather than on the activities, methods, and relationships of the learners. Teachers should remember that

the relation of events, especially remote in time, is difficult to make clear even to adults.

4. A teaching plan is not a collection of "juicy phrases" or points of importance. Unfortunately, some teachers look upon catchy phrases or even important points of truth as "collectors' items" to be brought to a class. No matter how clever or attractive these materials are, or how skilfully they are organized, they are still materials, and the mere presentation of materials is much less than good teaching.

Certainly the teacher must have something to say, and assuredly it ought to be something worth saying. Yet, a teaching plan is much more than a collection of good things to say. The "collection-type plan" implies that the teacher believes that he is the fountain of wisdom and his members are empty pitchers to be filled.

Some positive definitions clarify the matter.—If the foregoing negative considerations have eliminated some inaccurate concepts of the teaching plan, perhaps the following definitions will point up some of its distinctive functions.

1. A teaching plan is a guide to a higher quality of preparation. Unquestionably, many Sunday school teachers need to spend more time in lesson preparation. An even greater need is that of a higher quality of preparation. Preparation must do more for a teacher than provide him with an abundance of material for the thirty minutes that he "stands before his class," which, incidentally, he should not do, for better teaching is more readily accomplished when the teacher is seated with the class in an informal arrangement.

Good preparation gets beyond the general into the realm of the particular. No matter how many times a teacher has taught the lesson, he has never taught *this* class *this* lesson before.

Creating a teaching plan helps the teacher improve the quality of his preparation in several ways.

(1) It improves the teacher's concept of the teaching-learning process.

(2) It helps the teacher clarify and correlate his objectives.

(3) It broadens the teacher's background in the Bible material.

(4) It improves the teacher's understanding of the content and context of the unit of study.

(5) It simplifies the organization of appropriate learning activities.

(6) It enables the teacher to make the class session an adventure in discovering truth.

2. A teaching plan is the organization of learning activities. If a learner is to learn something well and remember it, he must discover that something for himself. Learning is a quest for understanding and meaning. Learning is seeking, searching, finding. Therefore, a teaching plan is the organization of the discovery activities of the members. Likewise, the better the teaching plan, the more the emphasis will be placed on the learner and the less on the activities of the teacher (in the class session).

Learning must be made meaningful to the learners. Therefore, the learning situation must be organized so that there is a maximum of opportunity for understanding, insight, and clarification. These opportunities are the foundation of a good teaching plan. It is not enough for a class member to *know* a fact, truth, or principle—even those of God's Word. He must also discover its meaning, its connection with life, its relation to other truth, and its applications to Christian experience. Therefore, the teaching plan must provide for making Bible truth practical, personal, and experience-centered. These requirements call for comprehensive, specific thinking ahead—much as an architect prebuilds on paper the structure he anticipates. This does not mean that changes will not be made. It does mean that the learning activities will not be spontaneous, irrelevant, and meaningless.

3. A teaching plan is a psychological procedure for the class session. To organize learning activities in a psychological manner does not mean or imply trickery or manipulation of the learners. It simply means that the learning activities and materials are arranged in the easiest and most natural way. A

psychological plan also suggests that the truth to be learned should be adapted to the ability, experience, and need of the learners. Bible truth must also appeal to the interests of the learners.

Because the interests, needs, and abilities of the learners are interrelated, it is quite possible to harmonize each of these with the lesson content. Although it is possible that all of these factors may not necessarily be included in every plan, it is certain that they must all be considered if learning is to occur.

A psychological teaching plan is one that meets the requirements of the mind and the needs of the learners. Obviously, individuals learn all types of material in their own unique ways. Therefore, the Sunday school teacher who works in harmony with the laws of learning will teach more effectively, even though he is teaching inspired revelation.

The thesis of this book is based on the premise that a psychological plan of teaching is both a Christian and an intelligent approach to learning. Therefore, the basic principles suggested in succeeding chapters are in keeping with this point of view.

What Does a Teaching Plan Contain?

Each teaching plan will vary in content and somewhat in form. Since teaching cannot follow a static pattern or routine, there can be no single approach to the making of the teaching plan. Although each teacher eventually finds his own general style and format for writing out his plan, he likely never uses the identical procedure twice.

On the other hand, if one works in harmony with the principles of learning, his plan must of necessity incorporate certain basic steps that grow out of these principles.

At this point a brief overview of the teaching plan is presented, but it should be emphasized that one step of the plan is not necessarily completed before another is begun. It is often true that several phases are developed simultaneously or concurrently. Particularly is this the situation with reference to the Bible study activities and the personal considerations of the truth. Whatever format the teacher follows, if it is to guide learning, it must grow out of his knowledge of the principles of learning, of the lesson, and of the learners. In addition, the teacher must take into account the interrelationship of these factors in the learning process.

The steps or phases presented here, and elsewhere in this book, are listed in a psychological order and in successive steps, because this approach is the only logical way to study the separate parts of an integral whole.

The first section sets the direction of learning.—A look at the picture of the teaching plan work sheet following page 103 reveals that the first side of the plan includes only the general guiding idea; the basic direction the lesson is planned to follow. There are three significant factors in establishing the direction of learning.

1. The major truth of the lesson must be identified.

2. The needs of the members, toward which the lesson can be slanted, should be spotlighted.

3. The teaching aim for the lesson must be determined.

All of the teacher's preliminary reading and all of his specific preparation converge at the point of finding the direction that learning should take.

The second section outlines the activities for learning.—Not only must the teacher discover the direction of learning, he must also organize the activities for learning. These activities constitute the remainder of the teaching plan and grow out of the findings of the first section.

Four specific activities are needed to complete the plan.

1. Plans for stimulating interest in the lesson and making a natural transition to Bible study

2. A major activity or framework around which purposeful Bible study may be built

3. Personal considerations that bring Bible truth "home" to the learners and practical activities that help the learners accumulate truth and challenge them to put their new insights and decisions into actual practice

4. An activity for stimulating the learners to study the next lesson

Each item mentioned in both sections of the teaching plan will be treated more comprehensively in the separate chapters which follow.

How Does a Teaching Plan Implement Learning?

Timeworn and trite, but singularly true, is the old adage, "Experience is a dear teacher." In fact, all learning comes from experience. Yet, all experience does not necessarily result in effective learning. The effectiveness of learning depends on the meaningfulness of the learning experience to the learner. Meaningfulness depends upon involving the learner in a situation which is real and worthwhile to him. This kind of involvement grows out of thoughtful planning and a skilfully created teaching plan. In other words, the teaching plan has much to do with the accomplishment of learning, not in just a vague, mechanical sense or even in a magical way. Learning is aided by a good teaching plan because the making of a plan stimulates the teacher to take into account the essential factors in organizing and guiding learning.

The teaching plan fortifies the relationship between lessons.— A casual observation of the average teacher on Sunday reveals a serious lack of attention to the relationship between Sunday school lessons. How can the use of a teaching plan remedy this situation?

1. The teaching plan relates the lesson to the current unit. A good teaching plan begins with a review of the unit title and the unit aim. Therefore, when the teacher prepares a teaching plan, he automatically disciplines himself to reconsider the unit, its purpose, and the part the immediate lesson has to play in achieving the unit aim.

Units are formed by grouping together lessons which collectively present one major learning goal. When teachers teach lessons without relating them to the unit learning goal, they lose the cumulative value of the unit, thereby making learning fragmentary if not meaningless.

The regular, effective preparation of a teaching plan is the teacher's best safeguard against piecemeal teaching and the haphazard learning that results.

2. The teaching plan relates the unit to the lifelong objectives of teaching. Any teaching plan should pinpoint the life needs of the class members and relate these needs to the lesson. Because learning is a developmental matter, a continuous process, it is impossible, with any given unit, to meet fully the needs of the learners. Many similar units and learning experiences will be needed.

Therefore, at all stages of life each learner will have continuing needs which grow out of the process of development. These basic needs are incorporated into the objectives of teaching in order to provide an axis around which each unit revolves.

It is at this point that the teaching plan enters the picture, for it helps the teacher relate units of Bible study to personal development. By keeping the teacher conscious of both the units of learning and the objectives of teaching, the teaching plan plays a vital role in strengthening the relationship between lessons.

The teaching plan co-ordinates the basic factors in the learning situation.—Learning does not take place in a vacuum. It cannot be turned on and off at will. Each factor involved in the learning process is dynamic and active. These factors work either in harmony or discord with each other. Therefore, co-ordination of these factors is essential to best learning.

The teaching plan is a tool for bringing the factors of learning into a harmonious relationship.

1. The teaching plan provides a proper relationship between the learner and the Bible. Thoughtful teachers have long wondered how they might embody Bible truth in terms that are important and compelling to the learner. Some have sought to accomplish this by placing their total emphasis on "teaching the Word," that is, giving the full attention to "handing forth the Word of Life." They have failed to recognize that learning is not often achieved simply by saturating the learners with truth. These teachers forget that one does not learn until the material has been made meaningful to him.

Other teachers have sought to solve the problem of the relationship between the Bible and the learner by placing their total emphasis on the learners' experiences.

There is unquestionable merit in both of these approaches; yet neither has proven to be fully successful. A balance between the two is needed. There is always value to the learner in content, especially when it is the inspired Word of God. Also, the fact that learning takes place through personal experience is of utmost importance. The crux of the matter is how can the teacher turn into spiritual nourishment the learners' personal experiences with the Bible?

The use of a teaching plan helps the teacher plan learning activities which have purpose and value for the learner. Yet those purposes are always geared to seeking, searching, and discovering Bible truth and its meaning. Perhaps an oversimplification will illustrate the point: A teaching plan helps the teacher teach the learner the Bible but not to teach the Bible to the learner.

2. The teaching plan correlates Bible truth and learning activities. The preparation and use of a teaching plan simplifies the task of selecting activities that facilitate the learning of Bible truth. For example, the right use of a teaching plan all but makes it impossible for a teacher to spend the whole class time *telling* the members what he ought to have them *discovering* for themselves.

Helping class members learn involves some telling, some asking, and some showing on the part of the teacher. However, the greatest values in teaching come from pupil activity. This is the reason why a teaching plan is of such great value. It is prepared with a view toward guiding learners rather than telling listeners.

The teaching plan follows the principles of learning.—Learning is not an uncontrollable, haphazard thing. Rather, learning grows out of the proper use of certain principles. Although some educators hesitate to speak of "laws" of learning, they are in unanimous agreement that there are some basic principles that govern learning.

These principles of learning have been frequently stated in a variety of forms, but essentially these statements are in agreement with the following:

1. A readiness for learning must be induced.
2. An element of discovery must be introduced.
3. A personal involvement of the learners must be motivated.
4. The truth must be assimilated and incorporated.

A good teaching plan not only includes each of these principles; it is built around them. It is obvious then that a teaching plan is not a document containing all that a teacher will say in the classroom, but rather it is a specific and practical procedure for guiding the learning activities of the members.

Thus, the teaching plan is a valuable aid in applying the principles of learning so that every class session can become an exciting adventure in bringing together the experiences of the members and the truth of God's Word.

How Is the Teaching Plan Used in the Classroom?

Any task well planned is well on its way to completion. For this reason the teaching plan is the best guarantee of an effective class session. Certainly the teaching plan does not make teaching an automatic, routine matter. On the other hand, the teacher who has climaxed his preparation with the creation of a good teaching plan knows where he is going and can face the class session with confidence and enthusiasm. He is free from the worry of finding something to say, because he knows what he is going to get accomplished.

What are the classroom functions of the plan?

The plan stimulates the teacher's memory.—Some few fortunate persons may be able to commit to memory a teaching plan week after week, but the vast majority cannot do so. Actually, the teaching plan makes such feats of memory unnecessary. It also leaves the teacher free to concentrate on the developments in the classroom rather than on trying to recall "where he is" on his plan. Since the plan is built around things to *do* more than things to *say,* the teacher's need for a memory prod is limited to ideas and activities. Memory aids of this nature are not only sufficient but are actually more efficient.

The teaching plan releases the teacher from being a slave to his notes and allows him to become the "master" of the situation.

The plan expedites the learning experience.—As the teacher prepares his teaching plan, he seeks to prelive the learning activities. As he uses his plan in the class session, he follows it as a guide in the actual experiences of learning.

As the teacher follows his learning guide plan, he does not coerce the learners into a preconceived mold but simply uses it to help them find the most satisfying and fruitful path to learning.

It is obvious that no one can fully predict the best path to learning, but the teacher who *plans* best *adapts* best to necessary changes en route. Having been over the ground before through the preparation of a teaching plan, the teacher is able to guide the learning experiences simply by referring to the "map" of the terrain the class is expected to traverse.

The plan insures flexibility in procedure.—As has already been implied, the teaching plan does not require strict adherence to its proposals. Learning in a stiff, formal, stereotyped manner is forced if, indeed, it occurs at all. The teacher must be constantly aware of the need to adjust his teaching procedure if learners are to learn. However, it is rather ridiculous to expect real learning to occur if no one has explored the possibility through advance planning.

When a teacher uses a teaching plan he is not trying to get off a ready-made lesson but is fitting to individual learners a tailor-made experience.

The teacher who follows a "bringing the lesson" routine is so concerned with the lesson content that he uses the learners simply as a sounding board. Only by following a prepared teaching plan can a teacher become flexible enough to organize learning experiences and guide the learners through them.

The right kind of teaching helps learners discover the truth and its meaning to them. To accomplish these results, the teacher must be able to adjust, digress, or even occasionally abandon his intended approach. Yet, he will not be able to cope with these situations without a teaching plan. If he is to achieve any measure of flexibility in meeting unexpected developments, the teacher must acquire skill in using a teaching plan.

The plan simplifies the attainment of response.—Intelligent response, growing out of personal participation, is the eventual key to learning. Most learners have difficulty clarifying their thinking unless they are able to "vocalize their confusion" and state their concepts. Participation, therefore, must not merely be *allowed;* it must be *secured.* It is not enough to permit learners to "tell what they got out of it." They must be encouraged and stimulated to participate thoughtfully and in a responsible manner.

The teaching plan includes, not only time for participation, but activities which foster it. Using such a plan not only keeps the teacher aware of the necessity of participation in learning but, at the same time, provides a visual reminder of the participation he has planned to provoke.

The plan influences the pace of the lesson.—One of the most difficult achievements in teaching is the ability to pace the lesson wisely. It is not easy to plan the proper amount of time to be given to any particular part of the lesson, and it is even more difficult to keep the lesson moving at the proper pace. Yet both the response of the learners and the progress of the lesson must be carefully timed if the best learning is to be achieved.

Careful planning and frequent checking will help the teacher develop proficiency in estimating the timing of the lesson. As he becomes more skilful in determining the best use of time, he will also become more expert in pacing the lesson. Thus, the teaching plan not only helps the teacher arrange "time zones" for the various parts of the lesson, but it enables him to adjust the pace to meet the learning conditions encountered along the way.

3

First Things First

Few teachers, even the best ones, are fully satisfied with the way they teach. Obviously, there is "a great gulf fixed" between the teacher's actual performance and his goal for teaching proficiency.

Although the teacher may earnestly desire to do a more effective job of teaching, he will find little improvement until he has acquired skill in lesson preparation.

Fruitful teaching demands, therefore, diligent study and conscientious preparation of every lesson. Hence, intelligent preparation is the master key to better teaching. In this sense at least, the teacher who makes the best preparation will have the most success. Likewise, the teacher who is willing to pay the price in mastering each lesson will enjoy a greater satisfaction in his work.

Preparation, in the broad meaning of the term, includes much more than the mastery of the current lesson. Because the broader considerations are beyond the purpose of this book, it is sufficient here to point out that the diligent preparation of each lesson is a necessity for the most effective teaching.

Both in the making of a teaching plan and in the actual experience of teaching, the quality of the teacher's preparation is the major difference between effective and ineffective teaching. To make adequate preparation then is to put first things first.

Create an Atmosphere for Study

Any situation is greatly influenced by its surroundings, atmosphere, or "climate." For example, the atmosphere surrounding a dining room plays a strong psychological role in helping diners enjoy their meal. Likewise, the atmosphere in which the teacher seeks to prepare and plan for teaching exerts a strong influence on the quality of his preparation. A good study atmosphere is the product of several factors.

Arrange suitable physical surroundings.—Although the surroundings may become so familiar and comfortable to the teacher that he ceases to be aware of them, nevertheless they dominate his attitudes. The teacher's zest for study, his enthusiasm about preparation, and even his attitude toward his class are greatly influenced by the surroundings in which he studies.

The conditions under which the teacher plans and prepares also affect the quality of the teaching plan. Study, like all intense intellectual effort, is tiring if not exhausting. To try to study in the midst of distractions, disorder, or disturbance is a practical impossibility for most persons. The product of such a study situation will be of a definitely inferior quality.

Not only should the study place be conducive to uninterrupted meditation, but it should also be properly equipped with a table or desk, books, teaching helps, and other necessary facilities for study.

Pray for spiritual guidance and mental alertness.—If teaching a Sunday school class is a spiritual ministry, then preparing to teach is a spiritual accomplishment requiring both spiritual guidance and mental alertness. The teacher who fails to pray earnestly throughout the course of his preparation invites disaster in the classroom. In addition, he misses the mental stimulation of his study and the joy of working in fellowship with the Holy Spirit. It is a great uplift to know that one is able to rely on the help of the same Spirit of God who inspired the Book that the teacher is preparing to help others learn. One's preparation must always be based on the guidance of the Holy Spirit.

The Sunday school teacher must remember that he is dealing with eternal issues and that the souls of his members are at stake. These responsibilities are much too sacred to be approached without the guidance and direction that come through earnest prayer.

Recall and evaluate last Sunday's session.—Preparation for any given lesson begins with an evaluation of the last one. In many ways it is unfortunate that Sunday school lessons must always be a week apart. Much of the cumulative value of preparation is lost because of this situation. Yet the teacher may partially overcome the handicap of intermittent sessions by learning to recall and evaluate the preceding class period.

It is at the point of recall that a teaching plan offers an important secondary value. It enables the teacher to review quickly and effectively the content of the previous lesson, think through the session, and evaluate its outcome.

Study the class roll and think about each member.—The effective teacher does not teach a class but individuals. Therefore, his preparation must include a careful consideration of each member. Even before the teacher begins to study the lesson content, he should get his class members in the center of his thinking. He should study his class roll name by name, thinking about and praying for each member.

The teacher who does not know his members well enough to recall their interests, needs, and abilities is certainly limited in his preparation as well as in his teaching, because he must teach *learners* rather than *lessons*.

The teacher who lacks this necessary information about his members can well afford to spend some amount of time in securing it. He could begin by making a subjective survey of his class, seeking to learn firsthand about the (1) spiritual condition, (2) home life, (3) school or business environment, (4) personality and temperament traits, (5) Bible and religious knowledge, and (6) special interests and abilities of each member.[1]

[1] See Gaines S. Dobbins, *The Improvement of Teaching in the Sunday School* (rev. ed.; Nashville: Convention Press, 1955), pp. 61–63.

Think through the progress in the current unit of study.—If real learning is to occur, the teacher must be aware of the progress the members are making in grasping the significance of the unit of study. As the teacher contemplates progress in the unit, he recalls what the members know, understand, and appreciate about the unit, how they are reacting to it, and what they are doing about it. These considerations form a background for preparation of the present lesson.

Bible truths, facts, and incidents are arranged into units of study so that they may become materials of learning rather than isolated data difficult to remember. Although the lesson writer bears the major responsibility for this organization of material, the teacher alone can make it meaningful and significant. Actually, he must make the *unit,* rather than the *facts,* become the real material of learning. Because of this fact, it is essential that an appraisal of progress be made as a part of preparation.

Master the Bible Passage and Lesson Treatment

Mastery of the lesson passage is far more than a general knowledge of the facts gained through reading the lesson treatment. Rather, it is the condition of having a thorough understanding of what the lesson *is* rather than what it *is about.* It is not enough to know what the lesson writers and commentaries have to say about the lesson passage. It is essential that the teacher master the original source, the Bible material, itself. More than a century ago Karl Lehrs laid down a rule for mastering a subject: "Always read sources; everything flows from them naturally." [2]

There are two important aspects of mastering the lesson content: first, a general, comprehensive knowledge of the Bible; and second, a specific knowledge of the particular lesson to be taught. Both of these areas of knowledge are essential. Yet a teacher may have an excellent understanding of the Bible but not know how to study a lesson in preparation for its teaching. Studying

---

[2] Gilbert Highet, *The Art of Teaching* (New York: Alfred A. Knopf, 1950), p. 94.

to teach means learning to master. What steps may a teacher take in mastering the lesson passage?

Read and reread the Bible passage.—Nothing helps one understand the Bible as much as reading it over and over while thinking, meditating, and praying for enlightenment. Not only can the teacher learn much about the Bible by reading in this manner, but what he learns will also mean more to him and be more valuable in his teaching. It is the difference between fresh, first-hand learning and wilted, hand-me-down information.

Certainly the teacher will need to read the lesson passage several times each day. He will want to read it silently and prayerfully. He will read it softly and meditatively. He will read it aloud and meaningfully. To gain further enlightenment and understanding he will read it from several translations and versions.

As the teacher reads, he should underscore, mark, and cross-reference the passage. He should look up the pronunciation of unfamiliar words. He should use a Bible dictionary to find the meaning and significance of names, dates, places, and so forth. The teacher should continue to read and reread the Bible passage until its meaning becomes so intensively alive and vital that teaching it will not be an effort but a positive delight to both himself and the class.

Make a simple outline of the printed passage(s).—After the teacher has become thoroughly acquainted with the printed portion of the lesson, he should make a brief outline of the passage, listing the major points and main subpoints. It should be emphasized that such an outline is not for teaching purposes but simply as a guarantee that the teacher's understanding of the passage is clear and logical.

Digest the background material in the teacher's periodical.— The best way to use the teacher's helps is to read, mark, survey, digest, and assimilate the information, thus making it a part of one's own thinking. Certainly the views of the lesson writer should be weighed and compared with those already gained from reading the Bible passage(s).

A most common error in preparing to teach is to begin study-ing by reading the comments of the lesson writers. As already indicated, one should begin with the Bible itself, leaving the teaching helps for later use.

Unfortunately, some teachers feel that they must learn all of the background material so that it can "be brought out in the lesson." To be sure, some of the background material will get into the lesson, but the main purpose of these helps is simply to supply the teacher with a backlog of the best resource ma-terials to enrich his own concepts and understanding.

In addition to the excellent teacher's periodicals produced by the denomination and provided by the church, some teachers try to find other helps. If the teacher has the time for wider study and the resources for purchasing additional materials, this prac-tice can be helpful within reason. It should be pointed out, how-ever, that this practice can be dangerous, especially for the in-experienced or untrained teacher, because it is easy to be led into error and confusion through the use of unsound literature. To borrow a well-known phrase from an investment firm, "investi-gate before you invest."

Write out a brief summary of the lesson.—Just as the teacher profits from outlining the lesson passage(s), he will also find it very helpful to write out a brief summary of the lesson. This written gist of the lesson need not include details, procedures, or applications but simply the broad contents of the lesson ma-terial.

Until a teacher is able to put his concept of the lesson into a clear, concise statement, he is not even ready to make a teaching plan, much less do an effective job of teaching. The value of writing out one's impressions to help clarify his thinking is no recent discovery. Almost three centuries ago, Sir Francis Bacon said that writing makes "an exact man."

Consult commentaries and books to verify conclusions.— Books and commentaries serve best as a check source on one's own conclusions formed in personal Bible study. To use them otherwise is to weaken rather than strengthen one's ability to understand the Bible. It requires a degree of patience and discipline to reach an opinion first and then verify or correct it by referring to recognized sources. Yet this procedure is what the best teachers follow.

The teacher who habitually relies on his books and helps to learn what the Bible says is making himself dependent on the thinking of others, failing to rely on the "Spirit of truth" and cheating himself of the joy of discovery.

Establish the Direction of the Lesson

Up to this point, the teacher's preparation has been purely subjective. He has been concerned with learning the lesson content and searching for its meaning. As he begins to contemplate the teaching of the lesson, he must determine the direction it should take. He must find a frame of reference out of which learning may emerge.

The teacher's concern is not how to cover the lesson but how to uncover it. The problem is what to do with the subject matter of the lesson—how to turn it into spiritual nourishment.

If the members are to learn and the teacher is to teach, finding lesson direction is a most important part of the process of preparation. Actually, this process of finding the lesson direction is the final stage of the teacher's personal preparation and the beginning stage of creating a teaching plan.

How may lesson direction be established?

Review the current unit of study.—The teacher must always keep in mind the essence of the current unit of study. It is the hub around which all meaningful learning is organized. In reviewing the unit the teacher may consider several questions such as: (1) What is the unit title? (2) What is the unit aim? (3) How does the present lesson fit into the unit structure? (4) Does the unit stress Bible knowledge or Christian experience? (5) What has been the general response of the members to the unit?

As the teacher rethinks the unit of study in the light of his present preparation, he will usually begin to "feel" the general direction toward which the lesson should move.

Pinpoint the major truth of the lesson.—Although the teacher's periodical lists the lesson writer's concept of the central truth, it is best for the teacher to form his own statement of this truth. The truth should focus on the heart of the Bible passage(s) as it relates to present-day life.

Inasmuch as a later chapter deals more fully with the techniques of locating the central truth, it is sufficient at this point to emphasize that the direction of the lesson is vitally affected by this truth.

List the lesson-related needs of the members.—Although the classroom procedure must make the *interests* of the members the starting point in learning, the *needs* of the members are the starting point in finding the direction of the lesson.

As the teacher considers the needs of the members toward which the lesson should be directed, he states the needs as specifically as possible. Generalities such as "to live better," "to be more consecrated," and so on, do not establish the lesson direction; they diffuse and dilute the lesson. The members' needs, if they are to help determine lesson direction, must be stated pointedly, for example: (1) to look upon tithing as an expression of one's love for God; (2) to learn the difference between gratitude and thanksgiving; (3) to face the Bible's teaching on strong drink; and (4) to prepare for an intelligent and reverent participation in the Lord's Supper.

In listing the needs of the members the teacher should think of the individual members rather than of the class as a whole. It is the individual needs that the teacher must seek to meet. Therefore, they should be the needs that help determine the lesson direction.

Form an appropriate aim.—The formulation of the lesson aim is the final step in establishing the lesson direction. However, the aim itself grows out of the needs of the members as they are related to the central truth of the lesson. This means that the lesson is directed toward meeting the needs of the members as these needs are mirrored in the central truth and in the unit purpose.

Because the needs of any two classes are never identical, the direction of a lesson will be somewhat different for every class.

Prepare a Statement of Procedure

After the teacher has determined the lesson direction, he is ready to prepare his teaching plan. The first step is to prepare a statement of procedure. In some cases, an experienced teacher may not need to comply with the suggestion that a statement of procedure be prepared. Yet, to train oneself to do so is, indeed, a most helpful safeguard against being more concerned with having something to say than with having something to do.

The preparation of a statement of procedure should not be confused with the making of a teaching aim. The aim is a statement of the learning outcome that the teacher hopes to help his members achieve. The statement of procedure is a summary of what the teacher plans to do to enable the members to learn.

Although it will take patience to develop skill in stating the procedural guide, it will be a very rewarding experience for the teacher. Not only will the practice increase the teacher's ability to see the lesson in a concise form, but it will also simplify the making of a complete teaching plan.

There are four simple steps in creating a statement of procedure.

Make the statement from the teacher's point of view.—Since the statement is the gist of the teacher's personal activity in the classroom, it should be written out in terms of his own purpose. It should be stated in the first person. For example, the statement may begin, "I propose to . . ." or "I will endeavor to . . ."

Indicate the Bible truth the members must face.—It is not the teacher primarily that the class members must face. Rather, it is the major truth of the lesson text. Therefore, the germ of the truth should be included in the statement of procedure. For example, the previous statement may be enlarged to say, "I propose to confront my class with the fact that God requires personal righteousness."

Include the basic activity of Bible study to be used.—Recalling that the statement of procedure is the teacher's proposed activity, and that it includes the germ truth of the lesson, the teacher completes the statement by setting out the learning activity to be used.

To add once more to the example statement, it would be completed in this manner: "I propose to confront my class with the fact that God requires personal righteousness; therefore, I shall lead them to discover the main points of righteousness found in the experience of Amos."

Re-examine the statement for accuracy.—The conscientious teacher will want to improve his skill in forming his statement of purpose. After completing the trial statement, he will find it helpful to apply the following tests: (1) Does the statement indicate what the teacher proposes to do? (2) Is the statement written in the first person? (3) Does the statement pinpoint the major truth of the lesson? (4) Does the statement spotlight the basic Bible study activity to be used? (5) Does the statement grow out of the lesson direction which was previously established?

Plan the Learning Activities for the Class Session

The final part of the teacher's preparation is to plan the learning activities that will be introduced in the class session. This step constitutes the second section of the teaching plan and includes: (1) ways to stimulate a readiness for learning, (2) activities for securing purposeful Bible study, (3) plans for getting truth into life, and (4) methods for stimulating interest in the next lesson.

As these steps are developed, they are written into the teaching plan which, in turn, becomes the blueprint for teaching and learning.

Because these four steps constitute the basis of the last four chapters, they are only mentioned here to indicate the concluding phase of the teacher's preparation.

It should be emphasized that the wise and diligent teacher will plan with all of the intelligence, foresight, and insight he can muster. But he will at the same time pray constantly for the leadership of the Holy Spirit. No amount of preparation will make teaching effective unless "the wisdom that is from above" (James 3:17) enlightens the mind and heart of the teacher as he plans. On the other hand, even though the Lord can use an untrained, poorly equipped teacher, he uses best the teacher who conscientiously and prayerfully prepares to teach in harmony with the best known principles of learning.

4

On the Main Line

The teaching-learning process in some ways resembles a great railroad system. In addition to the main trunk line, there are numerous side lines, branches, and switching points. All of these extra tracks are important to a railroad, but the traffic must be kept on the main line if progress is to be made. Some passengers may enjoy side trips and excursions, but those who desire to get somewhere want to stay on the main line.

In teaching and in learning there are many interesting and inviting side issues. Excursions into these lands may prove interesting to the teacher, and even to some members. But when teachers and classes engage in the search for spiritual curiosities or "cunningly devised fables," they are prone to leave the main line of the lesson truth, and become sidetracked on issues that result in purposeless teaching, meaningless learning, and profitless class sessions.

The appeal for main line teaching does not imply that there must be no deviation from the teacher's plan for a given lesson. Some of the best teaching-learning situations are not predetermined. On the other hand, classes that follow the Athenian plan, "to tell, or to hear some new thing" (Acts 17:21), will never experience the joy of discovering Bible truth that has meaning and pertinence for Christian living. Teachers and classes that try to follow up every verse, word, or idea of the lesson find themselves lost in a pointless, frustrating hodgepodge.

The Bible is the Word of the living God, and it has power to make learners new creatures in Christ and new personalities through Christian nurture. Simply to engulf learners in a broad or even "deep" intellectual discussion of Bible matters, however, is not teaching, and it is more likely to add confusion to spiritual illiteracy.

Knowledge for the mind must be transmuted into food for the soul, and the teacher is committed to teach so that learners grow in spiritual maturity. Christian maturity comes through understanding and assimilating the Word, not through absorbing myriad details and verbalized shibboleths about the Word.

Teaching that produces spiritual maturity is more concerned with dynamic spiritual issues than with intellectual accomplishments. Even though such matters as Christian ideals, concepts, and insights are only outcomes of learning, they must be of primary concern in teaching. Otherwise, side issues become the main line of interest, and spiritual growth will be minimized.

What then can be done to keep teaching and learning on the main line?

Concentrate on One Truth in Each Lesson

Concentrating on one truth does not eliminate touching on a few other related matters, but it does imply that learning is more intense and more life-changing when Bible study is specific. There are several reasons for this.

Each lesson contains more than can be taught.—Probably every Sunday school lesson contains far more Bible material than can be used. However, the teacher should not feel guilty about not "covering the lesson" completely. Main line teaching is not nearly as concerned about covering the ground as it is about cultivating it. A thorough exploration of the one big idea in any given lesson is far more enjoyable and fruitful.

Probably the greatest weakness in the "read-a-verse-around-and-tell-what-you-get-out-of-it" approach is the very fact that there is so much in some verses and so little in others. Chapter and verse divisions were added to the Bible to facilitate locating passages. Some of the chapter and verse divisions are not logical, and they sometimes hinder the search for truth. Some verses have much truth while others have none in themselves, because several verses must be used together to get the truth.

The limitation of time prohibits full coverage.—Even if the class had enough interest and the teacher enough ability, it would be impossible in thirty to forty-five minutes to exhaust the truth in any given lesson. It is also true that many Bible truths and many good teaching techniques must, because of the time limit, be omitted from Sunday school teaching. Perhaps it is appropriate at this point to make an appeal for all Sunday schools to provide a minimum of forty-five minutes for the class session.

Better learning comes from selective study.—Learning is searching, discovering, and understanding the point rather than the details. Learning is not a mechanical process of being exposed to all of the facts but a dynamic process of finding meaning, insight, and comprehension of the main point. One big truth carefully and thoughtfully considered brings better understanding to the learners than any amount of detail chasing.

Learn to Identify the Central Truth

Since it is important to spotlight one major truth in the lesson, it is essential that the teacher learn how to identify the major truth. It is not difficult to master the technique of "truth detection." A few guideposts and some diligent practice usually bring success.

Rethink the lesson passage.—If necessary, reread the passage and think it through. What is the over-all emphasis of the passage? Is there one simple, outstanding idea toward which the entire passage points? If so, this idea is a good clue to the central truth.

Consider the lesson title.—After rethinking the lesson passage, the teacher should think about the lesson in relation to the lesson title. Just what does the lesson say about the title? What big idea does the title suggest? Is it the same idea that seems to stand out in the lesson passage(s)? Does the basic idea of the title suggest a specific Christian principle that is brought out in the lesson passage?

Check the Memory Selection.—Quite frequently the suggested Memory Selection will contain the key idea of the lesson. Does the gist or germ idea of the Memory Selection point toward the lesson title and lesson passage? Do these three ideas seem to agree basically?

Recall the unit of study.—The major truth of the lesson will be related to the title and basic idea of the current unit of study. What is the title of the unit? What is the unit aim? What is the big truth of the unit? Does the central truth under consideration coincide with the unit truth?

Analyze the lesson writer's stated truth.—The lesson writer's idea of the central truth is always helpful. However, the teacher should first decide for himself what he thinks the central truth is. The lesson writer's idea is most useful as a check point for the teacher. Discovering the major truth will also prove to be far more helpful to the teacher than just accepting without question what the writer says. He will also find it helpful to ask: Is the writer's idea acceptable for my use? Can his statement be improved or simplified? How?

Convert the Central Truth into a Pilot Statement

It is not sufficient to have merely a general idea of what the central truth is. It must be a complete, comprehensive statement that can be used, evaluated, and written out. The following steps will help the teacher develop proficiency in writing an accurate statement.

Make the statement in one concise sentence.—Brevity and clarity are characteristics of a good statement of the central truth. As a rule the statement can be made in one concise sentence, never more than two or three short sentences.

The following statement is a good one for a central truth, but it is long and wordy:

God, as he revealed himself to man, sought to make his will known by taking a hand in history. God still works in history and even in the lives of individuals as he seeks to accomplish his purposes. He uses many people and instruments to achieve his will.

This statement can be reduced considerably: "God has a purpose for nations and individuals that will be worked out by the instrument he chooses."

Notice that the essentials are contained in the second statement. Yet, it is short and compact enough to be remembered easily.

It would be a good exercise to write out a statement of the central truth and seek to reduce it to bare essentials. The statement given in the teacher's periodical may be used as a check. It is far better for the teacher to learn how to state the central truth for himself than simply to look for the lesson writer's statement. The teacher grows only as he learns to discover and to work out for himself the various items that make up the teaching plan.

State the truth as a general principle.—The central truth is not a summary or condensation of the lesson. It is actually a statement of a principle of Bible truth rather than a synopsis of the facts or incidents themselves, although the principle does grow out of certain facts or incidents. For example, a lesson titled "Results of Self-Indulgence," taken from Isaiah 5:11–24, includes these facts: Isaiah credited the degredation and punishment of Judah to the drunkenness, dissipation, and debauchery of the people. The principle growing out of these facts may be stated: "Self-indulgence always results in a judgment of God." This statement is a general principle of truth that is always applicable.

Use terms that allow specific applications.—General principles are difficult to learn and more difficult to teach. This is the reason that general principles need to be "open" enough to allow specific applications. Using the previous example as a basis, a more specific central truth may be formed: "Self-indulgence, whether it is national or individual, always results in a judgment of God involving both moral and spiritual consequences." Notice how the "national and individual" and the "moral and spiritual consequences" phrases make the statement quite specific.

Both the principle and its applications should be related to present-day life. It is not sufficient to relate the truth to the distant past; it must be thoroughly and completely up to date in its application. Because it is the principle [central truth] that must be learned, the facts and historic setting around it are important largely as a vehicle to carry the truth.

Keep the statement true to the Bible.—The principle contained in the central truth must always be derived from the Bible passage(s). It must be stated in harmony with the main line of truth in the lesson and with all other related Scripture passages. It would be an unforgivable malpractice to twist, wrest, or misrepresent the Scriptures in a so-called statement of the central truth.

Test the Selected Truth for Accuracy

The wise teacher never allows himself to become careless or superficial in the selection of the central truth. He must learn to look at his statement objectively, if not critically. Being willing to rearrange or even to rewrite the statement until it is as accurate as possible is essential to a good teaching plan.

Some tests that may be applied to the statement act as a safeguard and guide:

1. Does the statement reflect the heart of the lesson passage?

2. Does the statement pinpoint the idea suggested by the lesson title?

3. Does the statement set forth a basic principle of Bible truth?

4. Does the statement contain the gist of the Memory Selection?

5. Does the statement coincide with the unit of study?

6. Does the statement present an interest, problem, or need in present life?

7. Does the statement seem appropriate to your class?

8. Does the statement square with all of the teachings of the Bible on the subject?

Transfer the Statement to the Teaching Plan

When the teacher has found a satisfactory statement of the central truth, he should write it on his teaching plan as pictured following page 103. (A year's supply of this work sheet, along with other materials, is provided in a *Teaching Plan Kit,* published by Broadman Press and available at local book stores.)

Although the selection of the central truth is only the first step in preparing a teaching plan, it is a very important step in establishing the direction in which the lesson will move. It also identifies the one big principle of Bible truth that each member of the class should be able to absorb as a result of his activities and experiences in the classroom.

5

Aim Before You Fire!

John Dewey once said that "acting with an aim is all one with acting intelligently." [1] Unless the hunter is content simply to hear the noise of his gun, he must aim before he fires. Unless the teacher is content simply to hear his own voice, he must have an aim before he teaches. An aim is to the teacher what an aim is to the hunter—"the direction of activity toward a foreseen end." [2]

It matters very little how expert a teacher may be in telling stories if the stories point in no particular direction. It matters very little how adept a teacher may be in provoking discussion if the discussion has no point. It matters very little how effectively a teacher raises questions if the questions lead to no particular conclusion.

Even though these procedures, and others like them, are essential in teaching, they make little contribution unless there is a definite aim or purpose in their use. Aimlessness and indefiniteness are the curse of teaching, because to teach in such loose fashion is to turn teaching into talking, activity into busy-work, and learning into incidental pastime.

---

[1] John Dewey, *Democracy and Education* (New York: The Macmillan Co., 1929), p. 120.

[2] C. B. Eavey, *Principles of Teaching for Christian Teachers* (Grand Rapids: Zondervan Publishing House, 1940), p. 46.

The aim is the most important and influential factor in the teaching plan. It is the axle on which the wheel of learning revolves. It is the stack pole around which the harvest of teaching is piled. It is the cable on which the bridge of learning is suspended.

Jesus Christ and the apostle Paul, the two greatest teachers of all time, were anything but aimless teachers. Jesus said, "I am come that they might have life, and that they might have it more abundantly" (John 10:10). He also said, "the Son of man is come to seek and to save that which was lost" (Luke 19:10). The writings of Paul are replete with advice, with admonitions, with definite aims. For example, "Study to shew thyself approved unto God, a workman that needeth not to be ashamed" (2 Tim. 2:15).

Indeed, teaching with an aim is old-fashioned, but it is not outdated. Teaching aims are ancient in concept but honorable in precept. Just as in times past the great teachers made sure of aims, today's teachers will teach better if they make use of aims. If teaching is to be fruitful and learning is to be meaningful, they must be organized around a focal point—an aim.

How Do Aims Improve Teaching?

The proper use of teaching aims enriches the entire teaching situation in several ways.

Aims provide a definite, orderly procedure.—Aims are directional in nature. That is, they direct the teaching-learning activities in an orderly fashion toward the accomplishment of the objectives of teaching and the goals of learning.

Aims also provide unity, coherence, and continuity of experience in an orderly and progressive search for truth. They help both teacher and learner to build on past experience and on existing foundations. On the other hand, aimless teaching is much like the antics of the butterfly, flitting from first one plan to another in a disconnected, haphazard, and illogical manner.

Actually, the aim is the very heart of the teaching-learning process, because it largely determines the results of the process.

On the surface, there may seem to be a great difference between the teacher who has only a hazy idea of "what teaching is all about" and the well-informed but aimless teacher. Yet, in both cases the results are the same—little or no learning is achieved.

Teachers who do not know how to make and use aims frequently find that their class sessions are little more than an abbreviation of the "forty years' wandering in the wilderness!"

It is a sad admission, but aimless, unfocalized teaching is quite common even in the most outstanding Sunday schools. Many teachers have made real progress in methodology but very little progress in the proper use of aims.

Aims allow a flexible learning situation.—Some advocates of ultraprogressive education want to indict as coercionists and manipulators teachers who use aims. Such an indictment is most unfounded. The use of a definite teaching aim no more requires a teacher to force his personal conclusions on a learner than a road map forces a driver to go to a particular city or a radar set forces a pilot to fly his plane on a particular course. In each of these instances, the only function of an aim, a map, or radar is to provide guidance and direction for arriving at a desired goal.

A teaching aim enables the teacher to organize the materials, activities, and situations in as meaningful a way as possible, but it does not preclude modifications or reorganization along the way. It would appear that the teacher who learns how to formulate and use an aim would be more able to adjust and adapt his procedure to changing conditions than would the teacher who had no purpose or aim. If this is not the case, it seems that a teacher who plans well but holds to his aim rigidly would still do better teaching than the teacher who has no aim or objective at all.

Teaching aims provide flexibility without flabbiness, definiteness without rigidity, and resourcefulness without extemporization.

Aims provide a criterion for selecting materials.—Sunday school teaching is concerned with the learner; yet it is also concerned with his relationship to the Bible. All of the techniques of teaching and the methods of stimulating and guiding the learners' experiences should grow out of the teacher's desire to make Bible study meaningful.

The teaching aim improves the teacher's judgment in the selection or rejection of the most useful materials and procedures for making learning meaningful and goal-directed. When the teacher has no aim, he is without any criterion or standard for making a choice of materials to be used or omitted. When the teacher has an aim, he simply selects the materials and organizes activities and situations that point toward the realization of that aim. He automatically eliminates those that do not relate to the aim, no matter how important or interesting they may be.

Teaching is never an end in itself. It must always be directed toward learning. So the clearer the teacher's understanding of the learning sought, the better is his selection of the means for achieving that desired end.

Aims serve as a means for evaluation.—Evaluation is an integral part of the teaching-learning process, because both the teacher and the learner must be aware of the progress they are making.

Even though the class members may not be able to state the teacher's aim, they are always aware of whether there is one and know in what direction it points.

Certainly the aim provides the teacher with a standard or norm against which he may determine direction and progress. Without an aim there is little basis for judging progress, because before progress toward a goal can be measured the goal must first be established.

Of course, there is much more to evaluation than that afforded by the measurement of progress in the light of the teaching aim. Nevertheless, this function is a highly significant value of a teaching aim.

How Do Aims Influence Learning?

Individuals learn within certain limits or focal points, not in general, wholesale fashion. Learning is a matter of "here a little, there a little" and is in many ways confused and disorganized.

Most modern educational psychologists agree on the need for unity in learning. They share this conviction because of the great difference between learning that is in sharp focus around an aim and that which is not. Learning is greatly improved when the learner is able to see reason and relationship in the things he is learning. To state it less technically, aims act as a great unifying factor in learning. They contribute to unity in several ways.

General objectives provide direction in learning.—General objectives, or long-range aims, are those that apply to the learner's continuing development and growth. They may also be called lifelong learning aims or all-inclusive aims.

The phrase "unto a perfect [full-grown, mature] man" from Ephesians 4:13 is generally accepted by the Sunday school as a lifelong aim for its members. A related expression in 2 Timothy 3:17 gives a motive for the lifelong aim: "That the man of God may be perfect, thoroughly furnished unto all good works."

All Sunday school teaching, therefore, is directed toward the building up in godly character of those who are taught. Since this ultimate aim is, in its fulness, impossible to achieve in this life, learners will need to be taught as long as they live.

All teaching and, consequently, all subordinate aims must, therefore, grow out of, point toward, and unify all learning in relation to the lifelong objectives of teaching.

As already indicated on page 14, a list of objectives for Christian teaching and training has been constructed to assist teachers in bringing unity and purpose into their teaching.

Quarterly aims unite broad areas of learning.—Quarterly aims are those that grow out of a series of studies, generally thirteen Sundays. Such aims serve to cement the lessons into a whole—a unit of learning.

The unit (quarterly) approach to study attempts to get the most from both the "whole" and "part" theories of learning. The unit approach recognizes that as one learns, he first grasps the big idea and then attaches details, not vice versa.

There is an interconnection and inner relationship between units of study, and these are tied together with one large aim for the quarter. In this respect the aim joins together into a functional whole the broad areas of learning.

Teachers who fail to understand the unit and its purpose do not use the quarterly aim to "bundle up" their teaching. Consequently, each separate lesson is taught as an entity in itself. There is little or no relation to the previous lesson or to the ones to follow. Thus, it is inevitable that many class members learn only in piecemeal fashion, and many teachers feel that their accomplishments are unsatisfactory. There can be little teaching or little learning under such a scattered assemblage of "lessons." It is the aim that gives unity and meaning to the broad units of study.

Unit aims identify learning goals.—The quarterly unit may have several smaller groups of units. There may be two to five of these subunits in any given quarter. Each of these smaller units constitutes a section of learning. The unit aim becomes, therefore, a learning goal for the small group of lessons. The adding together of these aims or learning goals constitutes a "whole" section of learning, which is the quarterly unit.

When the teacher recognizes the learning goals in the units, they become a foundation on which he builds a superstructure of learning. Otherwise, there is simply a disjointed, hodgepodge of miscellaneous material. Unit aims are the key to learning goals. Wise, indeed, is the teacher who takes advantage of them.

Lesson aims provide a learning focus.—Learning is an exploration, a search for truth and its meaning. Yet the search must be organized if meaning is to be found.

The lesson aim is the focal point of teaching and learning. It is the starting place in organizing the "search party." When there is nothing to be found, there is little reason to go on the search, and it is the lesson aim that pinpoints the object of the search.

There is a distinct difference between the members' going on a search for truth and in listening to a teacher recount his personal experience in finding the truth—as much difference as that between going on a bear hunt and listening to an illustrated lecture by a professional bear hunter.

The proper use of a lesson aim can make a like difference in teaching and, as a result, a like difference in learning.

How Are Aims Determined?

The teacher's periodical offers suggested teaching aims for each lesson. However, no matter how capable the writer may be, he will probably not be able to create an aim that is useful for all classes. In fact, each teacher will need to have a "tailor-made" aim for his particular class. Because no two classes are alike, it would be unusual to find any particular aim that would be equally appropriate for any two classes.

How then are aims determined?

Aims grow out of the central truth.—Although aims grow out of the central truth, they grow out of a particular aspect of it. The central truth is, as a rule, too large an area of truth to be fully covered by an appropriate aim.

Much thought and prayer should go into the selection of the right aspect of the central truth to be used as a basis for the aim. The type of Bible material, the size of the class, the unit of study, the age range of the class, and the needs of the members will play a vital part in the selection.

Aims are geared to the needs of the learners.—In determining the aim, the truth of the lesson is important, but the vital thing is what the learner needs that the lesson can supply. When a teacher does not know his class members intimately, it will either be the direct intervention of the Lord or sheer coincidence if he selects a good aim. Once again it is appropriate to point out that *learners* are taught rather than *lessons,* and the learners should be taught the truth they need. Aims must be geared to the specific needs of specific learners.

Learning to discover and identify needs is not too difficult. It requires time and patience, but above all it requires association with the members outside of the classroom. Probably the relationship between teacher and class member is the most important aspect of the whole teaching-learning process. This is certainly true with respect to the selection of teaching aims.

Perhaps it is unnecessary to point it out, but the fact that teacher and member must be closely associated if real learning is secured is the main issue in the appeal for a reasonable size in the enrolment for a Sunday school class.

Lesson aims are related to the unit and quarterly aims.— Lesson aims, though complete in themselves, are actually only a part of the whole. Each unit aim and the quarterly aim play a significant role in influencing the selection of the lesson aim. Obviously, the lesson aim should contribute to the learning goal set out in the unit aim. The lesson aim must also be related to the larger aim of the quarter.

It is not the size or importance of the subunit or quarterly unit that makes learning effective. It is the internal co-ordination brought about by the proper relationship of the various aims one to the other.

How Are Aims Stated?

A written statement of the teaching aim is essential both in clarifying the teacher's thinking and in the preparation of the teaching plan. It is one thing to have a general purpose in mind and quite another thing to have a specific aim on paper. Until a teacher can state exactly what he has in mind, he really does not have a usable aim.

To state an aim properly, at least three considerations are essential.

Aims should be stated from the teacher's point of view.— Since the teaching aim for any given lesson is simply a statement of what the teacher feels the class will need to learn, the aim should be written from the teacher's point of view. For example, "to help my members face the problem of . . ."; or "to lead my members to discover . . ."; or "to stimulate my members to appreciate . . ."

Although each of these statements embodies what the teacher hopes to see happen, let it be said emphatically that none of them involves forcing or eliciting predetermined responses from the members.

No teacher can always foresee what a learner may do in any particular learning situation, nor can the teacher accurately predict the specific outcome of any learning experience. But the teacher should know the basic needs of his members as they relate to any body of truth, and he ought to attempt to help his members with their needs in relation to that truth. If he is not to do this, what is the teacher to do? If he is not to do this, no authentic results can be expected, and the teacher becomes little more than a finder of consensus or a moderator over minutia.

The teacher's task is to influence his members and to help them face their own needs in the light of Bible truth. To fail to do so is not teaching, because teaching

is the exposition of the principle contained in the book; showing its connection with life, with action, with duty; making it the nucleus around which to gather all related facts and all collateral principles —it is this, and this only, which can appropriately be called teaching. All short of this is mere journey work, rude mechanical labor and drudgery.[3]

The teaching aim, therefore, should be a statement of the learning outcomes toward which the teacher will direct the learning activities and experiences of the class members.

Aims should be stated in terms of learning activities.—Although the teaching aim is stated from the teacher's point of view, it is not really an adequate aim unless it is stated as a learning activity of the members. It is always the learner who must learn, and he learns only through his own activity. Thus the teacher who secures learning must build his aim around definite learning activities of the members themselves.

To be stated in terms of member action, the aim must be beamed toward specific accomplishments of the learners. That is, the aim must include certain things for the learners to do and experiences to undergo. Action verbs are the key to a good aim. For

---

[3] Otis W. Caldwell and Stuart A. Courtis, *Then and Now in Education* (Yonkers-on-Hudson, N. Y.: World Book Company, 1924), p. 18.

example: to lead my members to *discover, feel, determine, apply, appreciate, give, experience, explore, understand*—these are words of action—action that the learners must take if they are to learn.

Aims should be stated in terms of desirable change.—Teaching must eventuate in changed learners before there is really any teaching, because teaching is a matter of life and living. "In short, true teaching is concerned always with the effecting of desirable changes in the one taught."[4]

As the teacher formulates his aim, he must think in terms of life adjustments because learning is changing. He must aim for desirable changes in the life of his members. He should aim to help his members (1) eliminate some things from their lives; (2) modify other aspects of their living; (3) strengthen the desirable things; and (4) develop those things that are lacking.

It should prove helpful to the teacher, when thinking about the aim to be selected, to consider these four questions: (1) What do my members need to discover from this lesson? (2) How do my members need to feel about this lesson? (3) What do my members need to understand about this lesson? (4) What do my members need to decide or do about this lesson?

For the lesson, "Results of Self-Indulgence" (Isa. 5:11–24), a sample teaching aim incorporating desirable changes may be stated: "To help my members face the evils of self-indulgence and to find ways to reinforce their resistance to the self-indulgent tendency of human nature."

Aims should be stated in concise form.—The teaching aim should never be a long and involved statement. It needs to be brief, concise, and simple. There are several characteristics of a good statement of the aim: (1) brief enough to be remembered, (2) specific enough to meet needs, (3) clear enough to be obvious, (4) practical enough to be attainable, (5) interesting enough to provoke participation, and (6) pertinent enough to undergird the unit.

---

[4] Eavey, *op. cit.*, p. 72.

How Are Aims Classified?

Aims serve to direct the teacher as he guides the learning activities of the members toward definite achievements. It would follow then that there would be about as many different kinds of aims as there are needs of the learners.

Since it would be impractical, if not impossible, to list the great variety of types of aims, some sort of inclusive classification must be made. One of the most popular classifications is that of Findley B. Edge: [5] (1) to teach knowledge, (2) to seek inspiration, and (3) to secure conduct response.

A practical but larger list would include (1) to teach new knowledge, (2) to increase understanding, (3) to enrich concepts, (4) to develop keener appreciations, (5) to improve attitudes, (6) to deepen convictions, and (7) to change conduct.

Too often teaching aims have been so general and so elementary that learning has been thwarted. There is a depth dimension in learning, a progressiveness in learning. To arrange a classification of aims in depth seems desirable.

Informational aims are basic aims.—It is always essential and basic for learners to discover new facts, information, and interpretations. These accumulations, however, are not really learning, because learning is changing, growing. The getting of information, a vital part of any class period, is simply surface learning and is readily forgotten unless it is made meaningful to the learners.

The tendency to forget unmeaningful information is illustrated by this experience. "Someone once said to the editor-in-chief of the *Dictionary of American Biography,* 'You must be one of the best informed men in America.' He answered, 'My mind is like a coal chute down which many tons of facts have rumbled, leaving only a little dust behind.' " [6]

Inspirational aims are affective aims.—The affective or emotional side of life is very important in teaching. Teaching aims of

---

[5] *Teaching for Results* (Nashville: Broadman Press, 1956), p. 97.

[6] Edward Hodnett, *The Art of Problem Solving* (New York: Harper & Bros., 1955), p. 42.

this nature are directed toward strengthening or developing attitudes, creating or deepening appreciations, developing ideals, and building convictions. Every aspect of teaching that is related to how a learner feels about a truth is very significant, because feelings and emotions play an important part in learning.

The inspirational or affective aims are directed toward a deeper level of learning than informational aims. Yet any feeling lessens as time dulls the memory of the response. Good teaching requires a reasonable appeal to emotion, but permanency in learning is not easily obtained with an inspirational aim alone.

Perceptional aims are depth aims.—Perceptional aims are directed toward the higher mental processes. When a teacher uses a perceptional aim, he strives to bring about such things as enriched concepts, thorough understanding, new insights, comprehension of meaning, relationships between truths, and assimilation of spiritual responses.

All real and lasting learning depends on the member's feeling that the learning matters to him and that it is intelligible to him; that is, it makes sense.

Probably most faulty Sunday school teaching lies in the fact that little use of perceptional aims has been made. Teachers have long given the facts, played on the emotions, and made general exhortations. But very few teachers have tried to teach so that every member of the class feels that the lesson "matters" to him and that it "makes sense" in a personal way. In other words, learners may know the facts but never understand what they mean—that is, they do not perceive. Without perception, learning is not intelligible, and when it is not intelligible, it has no meaningfulness. Consequently, the learning is soon lost. Actually, learning does not really occur until it reaches the perceptional level.

Motivational aims are action aims.—The motivational aims are those that seek to move the will of the learner so that action results. The motivational type aim seeks to help learners change, modify, or develop new conduct patterns; perfect new skills; improve their Christian practices; or engage in some definite corrective action.

In many ways learning depends on the will of the learner. Learning requires push and thrust. It cannot be achieved with a halfhearted, unconcerned involvement. The teacher must arouse and stimulate the will to learn. It is essential, therefore, that the teacher give attention to motivational aims if he desires permanency and action in learning.

It has already been indicated how aims should be chosen. Only a concluding admonition is needed. There needs to be a balance in the types of aims used. They are all useful and needed, but they cannot all be successfully used in every lesson. Certainly some accumulation of new information is inherent in any learning situation, but in addition to information the teacher, in most cases, will seek to bring about inspiration, or perception, or motivation. The wise teacher will major on one type of aim in each lesson, using only overtones of another type.

To use a teaching aim does not necessarily guarantee successful teaching, but to fail to use one will all but guarantee failure.

6

How to Begin

Plato has said, "The beginning is half the whole." Another word of wisdom on the subject comes from Euripides who said, "A bad beginning makes a bad ending."

Almost magical is the effect that the phrase "once upon a time" has on a child. Little other preparation is needed to assure his attention for hearing a story.

Teaching is another matter, however. Few learners have a strong motivation to learn. They have not been conditioned to begin learning at the sound of a phrase, the reading of a Scripture passage, or the asking of the question, "Does anyone know what the lesson is about?"

Learners must always be prepared for learning. This statement is as true of Bible study as it is of any other kind of learning. An intent to learn must be created; a readiness for Bible study must be developed if learning is to ensue.

How may the Sunday school teacher create a readiness to study the lesson? How may he arouse a feeling of need for learning?

Analyze the Reason for a Lack of Learning Readiness

Few learners ever bring to the classroom the appropriate attitudes and feelings that are conducive to real learning. Therefore, a learning situation rarely ever exists when the class first assembles, even when an excellent assembly program has preceded the class session. What causes this unhappy state of affairs Sunday after Sunday? Why is it essential that a state of readiness must be created for each lesson?

Recall the power of outside influences.—For at least 167 hours of the 168 hours each week, class members are under influences other than those of the Sunday school. It is unrealistic to expect that such influences will leave the members in the same frame of mind with the same interest in Bible study that they had during the last class session. Since the total impact of these influences is likely to be anything but spiritual in nature, class members are not generally prepared for diligent Bible study. It will be necessary for the teacher to help them develop both an interest in learning and a motive for learning.

Recognize the problem of preoccupation.—Class members of all ages arrive at Sunday school in a preoccupied state of mind. The social, athletic, recreational, occupational, and domestic experiences of recent days and hours have a tendency to linger in the thinking of the members.

The tendency toward preoccupation and even tension, turmoil, and conflict is heightened if the experiences have been highly emotional. Furthermore, an emotional state of mind all but destroys one's interest in learning. The sting of an unpleasant situation is a sure inhibitor of learning, and a preoccupied mind is indifferent to Bible study.

Thus, the teacher who fails to take into account these tendencies toward preoccupation may find himself unable to penetrate the learning barrier.

Respect the need for rapport.—Rapport means a satisfactory personal relationship between persons—a relationship marked by harmony, mutual respect, understanding, and confidence.

A feeling of rapport between the teacher and the members is essential to the teaching-learning process, because the emotional climate in the classroom has a strong bearing on learning. The mental and emotional state of the learner either releases or inhibits his energy for learning. Therefore, the personal relationships between the learning group and the teacher must receive immediate attention at each session.

Classroom climate and class rapport depend on much more than a good beginning for the lesson, but a good beginning is essential to learning and conducive to a wholesome classroom atmosphere as well.

Remember that learners must feel a need for learning.— Learners are selective in their learning; that is, they tend to learn only that which interests them, and the things that interest them are the things that they feel they need.

Certainly all learners need to learn more than they think they need. Fortunately, the very nature of the Bible, as it is studied, brings to the attention of the learners needs that were previously unfelt. Yet learning is enhanced when the teacher is able to set the stage for learning.

As the teacher contemplates a plan for creating a readiness for learning, he will recall as much as possible about the needs that his members seem to sense. To appeal to these needs, to begin on this level, and to seek to develop a feeling of need in new areas is a good technique in creating a readiness for learning.

Understand What It Means to Create Readiness

To assume that a class is ready to study the Bible as soon as it convenes in the classroom is assuming too much. To launch immediately into the lesson is to all but guarantee that most of the members will never make the journey to learning.

The prophet Amos posed a provocative question that all teachers need to ponder: "Can two walk together, except they be agreed [have an appointment]?" (3:3). This verse could be paraphrased, "Can two learn together, except they have an interesting point of beginning?"

Shakespeare was right when he said, "All's well that ends well." It can also be said that "all's well that begins well." No more appropriate remark could be made to emphasize that a good beginning in learning greatly aids a good outcome in learning.

To create a readiness is simply to "walk together" in learning, to "have an appointment" for learning. What must the teacher do to achieve this harmony of purpose and joint effort?

Establish a point of contact.—Some of the earlier twentieth-century educators referred to the finding of a common ground on which the teacher and learner might walk together as establishing a point of contact. This concept is not altogether appropriate but the germane idea of togetherness in learning is excellent. In teaching and learning there must be a point of beginning that is on the learner's level of interest and need. This point is, indeed, a point of contact. If there is ever to be any learning, there must be a sound and sensible contact established between the teacher and the class members.

Arouse interest in learning.—Any experienced teacher is painfully aware of the fact that few class members bring to the classroom a built-in interest in Bible study. Inasmuch as learning does not occur until the Scripture passage becomes meaningful, and since meaningfulness depends on one's interest in the matter, it is apparent that the teacher must arouse interest in the lesson if learning is to occur.

Actually, it will do little good even to begin Bible study until interest has been aroused. Indeed, beginning without interest could create a situation that would "teach" the class that Bible study is prosaic and perfunctory.

Since learning rarely results from study that is devoid of interest, it would seem that the teacher's first responsibility is to arouse and create a deep interest in learning.

Focus attention on the lesson.—The entire purpose of readiness building is to focus attention on the lesson. Therefore, any reasonable approach that directs attention to the lesson is usable and commendable.

Creating a readiness for learning is not to be confused with a mania for clever devices and schemes. Although creativeness is encouraged, a teacher should not become afflicted with "gimmickitis." There are many good devices and techniques in learning that are not appropriate for Sunday school teaching. The limitations of time, the character of the Bible, and the ability of both the teacher and the members preclude the use of some methods.

Relate the lesson to the unit.—Frequently the setting of the stage for learning should include a brief review of the unit and a tie-on of the present subject or area of study. Sometimes the reasons for studying the lesson should be given. On occasions, it may also be useful to disclose the teaching aim for the lesson and relate it to the unit of study.

Variety in beginning the lesson is most welcome. There should not be a set order or routine which the teacher follows regularly. Rather, he should seek for different ways to start the session.

Plan an Attention-compelling Approach

Learning to create an atmosphere of readiness is not too difficult, but it does take considerable thought and planning. Probably no two lessons should ever begin the same way; yet each lesson should use an approach that immediately secures attention. Someone has well said, "If you don't strike oil in three minutes, you may as well stop boring!"

There are many ways to stimulate interest in the lesson. Probably most of them can be incorporated into one of the following suggestions.

Share an appropriate story event or experience.—Storytelling has long been recognized as a good teaching technique. The story is also a valuable instrument for securing attention at the beginning of a lesson.

Relating or referring to some event, either current or historical, is also an effective use of the story approach.

The sharing of a personal experience is often the most effective way to begin a lesson; to ask the class "to pardon a personal reference" is certainly unnecessary. There is nothing a teacher can do that is more interesting than relating a personal experience.

Consider a specific "what-would-you-do" problem.—This technique is generally tagged as learning through a "life situation." Such a procedure is frequently pictured as the ideal way, if not the only way, to learn. This contention, however, raises some critical problems.

For what possible situation is there other than a life situation, including the most formalized of drills, and for that matter the memorizing of nonsense syllables? What is really meant, however, is that anyone learns best when the whole pattern of his life motives is engaged, and this is perfectly true.[1]

In using a "what-would-you-do" approach to introduce a lesson, either an actual or a hypothetical problem may be used so long as it requires a discussion-decision involvement. This is not an especially easy way to approach a lesson; therefore, the teacher should take several precautions. For example, the problem chosen should be a normal thing to expect in the lives of the members. It should offer alternate courses of action, one of which will spotlight the major truth of the lesson. The problem situation should confront the members with the necessity of discussing the various alternatives and finally making a decision about what should be done. Obviously the decision should come as a result of insight gained by studying the Bible lesson.

Analyze a verbal concept.—There is a wide field of opportunity in analyzing verbal concepts at the beginning of a lesson. A famous statement may be considered, a well-known quotation may be discussed, a proverb may be reviewed, or an adage may be given a proof-finding treatment.

In each of these approaches the basic purpose is to discuss the validity of the concept. It is not always necessary to prove or disprove the concept but simply to use it as a taking-off place for Bible study.

Use an appropriate visual aid.—Both projected and nonprojected visual materials are useful in beginning the lesson. Probably the most useful of all visual aids is the chalkboard. In fact, it may be said that the chalkboard is the best "assistant teacher" a class can have.

Maps, posters, objects, flat pictures, slides, models, diagrams, charts, graphs, and many other similar aids may be effectively used to get attention and to create interest in Bible study.

---

[1] Mursell, *op. cit.*, p. 52.

Raise a rhetorical question.—A good rhetorical question in some unique way draws teacher and learners together and compels them to accept an obvious answer or to realize that there is no apparent answer. Paul used this technique frequently in introducing a subject. For example, "Who shall separate us from the love of Christ? shall tribulation, or distress, or persecution, or famine, or nakedness, or peril, or sword?" (Rom. 8:35).

The use of such questions is intended to stimulate thinking that can be quickly directed toward the lesson.

Choose an Approach That Is Centered in Life

Learners are living in a very realistic world, and learning must begin where they are. A teacher should beware of trying to create readiness for learning by using an idea that is so heavenly-minded that it has no earthly meaning.

Arouse the natural curiosity.—Curiosity really means eagerness to know. It is the sign of a hungry mind. Curiosity is not a trait unique to cats alone, because all normal persons are naturally curious and inquisitive. Curiosity leads to interest, attention, and knowledge. An aroused curiosity is more important to learning than a placid memory.

Fortunately, even the existing interests form a basis for curiosity-induced approaches to learning. When there is no recognized interest, readiness for learning may be generated simply by judiciously arousing the curiosity of the learners.

Appeal to the emotional nature.—It appears that man is more emotional than rational; therefore, in leading him to learn it is important that he be emotionally involved at the very beginning of the learning experience. It is unwise to impose an emotional experience on a learner just for the sake of arousing the emotions. All emotional reactions need to be directed toward arousing an intent to learn.

Take advantage of built-in interests.—All learners have some existing, built-in interests that are natural and spontaneous. These interests may be used effectively by the teacher to stimulate class members to learn. It is, of course, invaluable for the teacher to discover and understand these interests, if he is to use them to create a readiness to learn.

Interest in recent events, world conditions, employment, community situations, and personal achievements are unending sources of material for setting the stage for learning.

Use an Approach That Stimulates Participation

Participation is not an end in itself. It is the road to learning, and every learner must travel it eagerly if he is to be successful in his search for truth.

Provoke vocal expressions.—It is generally easy to get people to talk, and there are many ways to induce participation when it is slow or difficult. However, the teacher should be careful to avoid becoming satisfied when his members simply talk. He may be developing skill in stimulating conversation but not really preparing his members for learning.

Certainly it is important to stimulate vocal participation, if members are to be prepared to learn. The vocal response reveals, not only the members' frame of mind, but also the depth of their readiness for real learning.

Involve the members intellectually.—Creating a readiness for learning requires more than a vocal exercise; it requires a mental exercise as well. The whole point of participation is to stimulate thinking, because there is no learning where there is no thinking. Even though there may be ample overt (vocal) participation, it must be deepened into intellectual involvements such as thinking, reasoning, weighing, evaluating, and meditating before a learner is truly prepared to learn. This is the covert phase of participation, but it is the very heart of the process of preparation for learning.

Help the members identify with the situation.—Individuals are ready to learn when they come to the place that they can identify themselves with the problem, situation, or activity under discussion. Actually, interest is basically the identifying of oneself with a situation that is personally significant, one that "makes sense" to the learner.

Obviously, a member is more interested in learning, understands better what he learns, and is able to use his learning more effectively, if he is able to "put himself" in the center of the learning situation.

Work for a Natural Transition to Bible Study

A compelling and stimulating beginning has only one purpose —to create a readiness for Bible study. Therefore, a natural, easy transition to the actual study of the lesson text is the outcome of a good point of contact.

Time the transition carefully.—The teacher will not be able to prejudge exactly the amount of time needed to prepare the members for study. As little time as possible should be used; one to three minutes is generally sufficient. However, there is a certain sensitiveness that he must develop—a "sixth sense" in teaching— that enables the teacher to sense the right moment to move the members toward the Bible study.

Practice and observation are the best tools for developing the ability to know when the transition time has come.

Make the transition smoothly.—The transition should be as smooth and natural as possible. Any abrupt change of pace or thought will distract attention rather than attract attention to the Bible.

The teacher's plan for the transition should be carefully made and written into his teaching plan, perhaps word for word.

The transition is the crucial point in the lesson. It must mobilize the energies of the members in a wholehearted attempt to master the lesson text, if learning is to be effective and teaching is to be fruitful.

7

The Berean Technique

It was reported of the Bible students at Berea that "these were more noble . . . in that they received the word with all readiness of mind, and searched the scriptures daily, whether those things were so" (Acts 17:11).

Most present-day Sunday school teachers are aware of a conflict raging between various groups of educators over philosophies of education. If one may be forgiven for oversimplifying the problem, it may be summed up as follows: the *traditionalist* believes that teaching should be concerned with the cultural development of the learner and that content and curriculum are extremely important; the *progressivist* feels that teaching should center in the social development of the learner and that content and curriculum are entirely expendable.

It is regrettable that these differing opinions creep into the views of Christian teachers to disturb those who want to do their best to teach their members the Word of God. On the other hand, every teacher has some basic philosophy of education, even though he may be unaware of its existence. And this philosophy exerts a tremendous influence on his teaching.

Teaching in the Sunday school is something highly related to, but greatly different from, secular teaching. Sunday school teaching should be concerned with the spiritual development of the learners; thus, content and curriculum are tremendously important means to such an end. It should be apparent that the divinely inspired Word of God is not ordinary content or curriculum. Its content is "profitable for doctrine, for reproof, for correction, for instruction in righteousness: That the man of God may be perfect, thoroughly furnished unto all good works" (2 Tim. 3:16–17).

Again, it is apparent that there is a real difference between cultural, social, and spiritual development, even though there are many overlapping similarities. In this case, the differences are more important than the similarities.

The Sunday school teacher must teach learners, but he must teach them the Word of God. It is a dangerous fallacy to say that content in Sunday school teaching is expendable. Bible knowledge is indeed a basic factor in Christian growth and spiritual development. The Bible is the content of Sunday school teaching—not the Bible as a social influence, though it does exert one; not the Bible as great literature, though it is the greatest of all literature; not the Bible as a treasury of wisdom, though it is that. Rather, it is the Bible as the "living and active" Word of life (Heb. 4:12, RSV) that is the content of our study.

The Sunday school teacher must keep his spiritual feet on spiritual ground. Teaching people the Word of God is the task of the Sunday school. Bible study is the reason for the existence of the Sunday school. Other things are good, even important, but the "thirty golden minutes" on Sunday morning are sacred. They must be unquestionably dedicated to Bible study. Just as those "more noble" Bereans of New Testament times "searched the scriptures daily, whether those things were so" (Acts 17:11), Sunday school teachers today must make Bible study the focal point of every teaching effort. The teaching plan must, therefore, center on purposeful Bible study.

Make the Class Period a Genuine Study Situation

Real study always involves investigation, exploration, searching, and discovery. Learning is a quest. Too few class sessions are actually characterized by real Bible study. Rather, they are more nearly described as a telling-listening marathon. This fact could be facetiously expressed as follows:

> Mary had a ladies' class,
> It was the worst one in the town;
> 'Cause Mary never learned to teach,
> She just talked 'til she ran down!

How may the class session become a genuine study situation?

Resist the temptation to deliver ready-made lessons.—Most Sunday school teachers fall back on the timeworn procedure of either speaking on the subject of the lesson or discussing the meaning of the verses in the lesson. Both procedures are weak and ineffective, because they do not require the learners to acquire any acceptable mastery of the Bible lesson. The exclusive use of telling and explaining not only relieves the members of any personal effort but also actually encourages them not to learn, because there can be no real learning without personal study.

When a teacher learns to resist the "hand-me-down" approach to teaching, he is able to lead learners to discover truths rather than to tell them facts. He is able to plan the things learners must do to learn rather than plan what he should say about the lesson.

Use a classroom arrangement suitable to study.—Classroom environment plays a most important part in learning. For example, a well-located, neatly kept, and appropriately furnished room suggests strongly that Bible study is vital and urgent.

The classroom arrangement contributes both psychologically and practically to the learning situation. For instance, a table serves as a unifying factor and psychological support, especially for reserved or timid learners. Again, participation and communication are greatly improved when the seating arrangement is circular or nearly so.

Admittedly, there is nothing magical about the arrangement of chairs, tables, and equipment; yet there is ample evidence that these informal arrangements make participation more vigorous and learning more meaningful.

Even the position of the teacher plays an important part in making Bible study effective. Whether the teacher "stands before the class" or sits with the class is important. Standing magnifies the teacher; sitting magnifies teaching. Standing implies authority; sitting implies togetherness. Standing motivates telling; sitting motivates sharing. Standing inhibits participation; sitting encourages response.

Stimulate the members to share the responsibility for learning. —There is an interesting sidelight in the meaning of the word "disciple." It comes from the Latin *discere* which means "to learn." The implication is that a learner must discipline himself if he is to uncover truth. In the final analysis, genuine learning is self-learning, self-discipline. How ridiculous it is, then, to place on the teacher all of the responsibility for learning.

On the other hand, even though learning is personal, the teacher bears an extremely important role in helping members learn. The role is one of stimulation and challenge. Members must be challenged and moved to accept their own share of the responsibility for learning.

Perhaps the greatest count against the constant use of the lecture is that it inhibits and destroys the will to participate. It turns a hungry mind into a flabby storage bin.

Teachers may stimulate members to accept responsibility for their own learning by helping them recognize needs, problems, and deficiencies, and by helping them achieve a satisfying experience of involvement in discovery. It is a truism of education that the more a teacher does for the learner, the less the learner does for himself. Within reason, it is true that the teacher should do more to stimulate learners and less to inform learners.

Make the class session an adventure in discovery.—Learning is always a process of discovery. It requires wondering, seeking, searching, solving, clarifying, and understanding. This fact means that teachers should tell their members as little as possible and lead them to discover for themselves as much as possible. In other words, the class session should be an adventure in the discovery of Bible truth and its meaning.

Turning the class session into a discovery time requires the use of learning activities. Therefore, the teacher must plan for, and lead the members in, a serious study situation. This statement does not give the slightest implication that the class is to become a monotonous academic routine. The quest for truth can and should lead up many interesting and exciting pathways.

Master the Technique of Purposeful Bible Reading

The reading of the lesson passages is always essential to the intelligent study of the lesson. However, the best results are obtained when preparation is made for the Bible reading. This means that the lesson passages should be read purposefully. Planning to get the members ready for reading the lesson text is an extremely important part of the teaching plan. How may this be accomplished?

Search for specific information.—Possibly the most frequently used approach to purposeful reading of the Bible is the searching technique. The teacher may propose that pertinent facts, truths, ideas, and points of view be discovered. For example, in reading Isaiah 61:1–3, the class may be divided into two groups. One group may compare Luke 4:18–19 to discover how Jesus used the Isaiah passage in the synagogue at Nazareth. The class could then correlate the two passages.

Settle a real or imaginary issue.—One of the most fruitful ways of getting the Bible read with purpose is to raise a question that can be studied in the light of the lesson text. This approach to purposeful reading helps class members develop the habit of using scriptural answers to settle all questions.

In studying Luke 1:26–35, the teacher may indicate that since there have always been some who argued against the incarnation of Christ, it would be profitable while reading the passage to list each fact found there that answers the question, "Was Jesus really born of a virgin?"

Reconcile differing points of view.—Another way to use the "issue technique" in getting the lesson text read purposefully is to point out opposing points of view and seek to reconcile them as the passage is read. For example, the opposing views on Christian "perfection" may be pointed out; that is, some claim perfection, and others say perfection is impossible. In studying Ephesians 4:11–13, the class may read the text with the purpose of reconciling these two divergent points of view.

Justify an opinion or belief.—Again, purposeful Bible reading may be stimulated by stating an opinion to be justified. This approach may be illustrated in the study of Paul's voyage to Rome. The teacher may state that a Christian's faith is not really valid until it has been tested by the storms of life. In reading the lesson passage, Acts 27:1–2,8–15, the statement can be carefully analyzed.

Plan Learning Activities That Require Exploration

The teaching plan is actually a blueprint of the things the members must do to explore the Bible passage(s). However, the amount of material and the limitation of time make it impractical to explore fully all of the truth in any given lesson. Therefore, the study must be purposeful, that is, limited to a certain area of exploration. This restriction requires the teacher to explain what the learners are to do, demonstrate how they are to do it, and allow time for them to do it. This kind of study is guided Bible study—a stimulating, inspiring, and helpful approach to the study of God's Word. But it is a kind of study that requires thorough planning and careful selection of learning activities.

Recall the basic activities of learning.—Activities that produce real learning are many and varied; yet they may be classified in six basic categories, each of which is highly useful in guiding purposeful Bible study.

1. Audio activities—listening to Bible truth through stories, questions, reading, experiences, assignments, brief periods of lecture, and recordings.

2. Visual activities—looking for Bible truth on the chalkboard, posters, pictures, photographs, drawings, objects, maps, charts, graphs, pamphlets, letters, books, projected materials, and various translations of the Bible.

3. Vocal activities—discussing Bible truth by asking and answering questions, reading the Bible, expressing opinions, disagreeing, clarifying ideas, memorizing, explaining, and praying.

4. Intellectual activities—thinking about Bible truth through meditation, reasoning, reflecting, accepting, rejecting, evaluating, deciding, applying, and problem solving.

5. Emotional activities—reacting to Bible truth by displaying love, friendliness, hostility, understanding, sympathy, helpfulness, and personal identification with Bible people.

6. Experimental activities—using Bible truth in study guides, books, concordances, maps, Bible dictionaries; making reports, records, notes, summaries, outlines, comparisons, and contrasts; doing research, group study, and learning projects; getting interviews; going on field trips.

Select activities that are appropriate.—In many ways teaching may be looked upon as the guidance of learning. Because each person learns in his own characteristic way, it will be necessary for the teacher to understand, not only the most appropriate activity for learning a given truth, but also the most appropriate activity for each learner.

It is readily seen, therefore, that the selection of the proper learning activity is not a simple matter. Some guidelines are needed. For example, the teacher must consider (1) the age and sex of the learners, (2) the degree of motivation that the learners possess, (3) the type of Bible material to be learned, (4) the members' present knowledge of the subject matter, (5) the kind of result sought, and (6) the needs of the learners.

To develop skill in determining the learning activity to be used, the teacher could prepare for his own class a chart of the most useful techniques. Perhaps the chart would be more practical if it stated the activities as questions and grouped them according to the desired changes. For example:

1. To gain knowledge: What passages should the class read? What visual material should the class view? What information should the class be given? What questions should be discussed? What reports or assignments should be heard?

2. To aid understanding: What problem should the class solve? What demonstration should the class evaluate? What discussion should the class pursue? What experiment should the class try? What small group study should the class undertake?

3. To improve attitudes and appreciations: What inspiration should the class experience? What reading material should the class follow? What kind of counseling should the class have? What type of discussion should be provoked? What dramatic experience should the class have?

4. To create interest: Which story or illustration should the class hear? Which questions should the class answer? Which challenge should the class face? Which role should the class see played? Which study guide should the class follow?

Use the same learning activity in a variety of ways.—It is quite apparent that more than one learning outcome can be achieved with the same activity. For example, discussion is an effective activity in almost any kind of learning situation. Questions, illustrations, and visual aids are highly effective regardless of the desired learning. Certainly Bible searching and reading are the basic activities of learning and teaching in the Sunday school class.

Combine activities for deeper impressions.—Just as most activities are useful in several types of learning, a combination of activities adds depth to the learning impression. Probably each major truth to be learned should be explored through a series of related but different activities. By using a combination of activities, the teacher may in several different ways confront the learners with the same truth. For instance, the class members may be led to read a truth from the Bible, do research to discover its meaning, hear it explained, discuss it, see it illustrated, and react emotionally to it. This "piling up" of experiences provides more than participation; it causes personal involvement which is essential to creative teaching.

Organize the Lesson Around a Major Bible Study Technique

The effectiveness and success of any job of teaching are heightened by a discriminating use of one major study technique for each lesson. Assuredly, there will be a variety of activities and methods, but there needs to be a "stack pole" on which they all lean.

One major requirement for significant learning is that the learner be as fully aware as possible of the results he is attaining. This fact emphasizes the need for a major Bible study activity which, even to the least interested learner, is an obvious necessity to learning.

An emphasis on organizing a lesson around one major study technique should not in any way be construed as a suggestion for wresting or perverting the Scriptures. Learning is rarely easy, nor does it occur as a matter of course; it is a result of concentrated effort. Therefore, to avoid confusion, to prevent undue digression and intensify impressions, the teacher should build the Bible study around one major activity. Regardless of the activity used, it should provide as much firsthand contact with the Bible content as is possible during the allotted time.

Confront the learners with a life problem.—A human being is a dynamic organism; that is, he is a living, moving, acting being. Merely to be alive is to experience numerous needs, whether or not they are consciously felt. Growing out of an awareness of these needs is an urge, a motive, or a drive to satisfy the need. If the need is satisfied easily and without effort, there is no learning. If, on the other hand, the need is difficult or challenging, it becomes a problem, and any conscious effort to solve the problem results in learning.

Successful Bible teaching begins by arousing within the learner a sense of need. Jesus used the Samaritan woman's need for water to create an awareness of her need for "living" water. In much the same way, Christian teachers must guide their class members through activities that help them meet the spiritual needs which grow out of life's problems.

For example, in studying the lesson, "The Search for True Values" (Eccl. 5), the teacher may confront the class with a life situation by asking, If you could have whatever you desire most of all, what would you choose? After a brief listing of responses, the teacher may suggest a series of experiments to find the best answer to the problem. The chalkboard could be used to list the experiments and the conclusions of the wise man as the members explore the Bible passage to discover them.

Experiments	*Conclusions*
1. Accumulation of knowledge (Eccl. 1:13)	1. Results in vexation, sorrow, and grief (Eccl. 1:16–18)
2. Pursuit of pleasure (Eccl. 2:1a,3,8)	2. Pleasure ends in emptiness (Eccl. 2:1b–2)
3. Search for fame and fortune (Eccl. 2:4–10)	3. Achievement brings no satisfaction (Eccl. 2:11,17–23)

Follow a special study guide.—The study guide sheet is one of the most interesting and useful devices for keeping Bible study geared to one major learning activity. Although study guides are very flexible and may be used with almost any kind of lesson, they are most helpful when they deal with relationships, attitudes, and appreciations. The study guide will need to be prepared in keeping with the lesson aim and designed to get the Bible passage(s) studied vigorously. A sample study guide follows.

Study Guide

LESSON TITLE: "Measured by the Golden Rule"
BIBLE MATERIAL: Matthew 7:1–12; Luke 10:25–37

1. Should a Christian judge others? _____ If so, when is he qualified to judge? _____
2. What risk does the Christian run when he criticizes others? _____ _____ (Matt. 7:1–2)
3. List the ways in which a Christian should use spiritual discretion. _____ (Matt. 7:3–6)
4. What resources does the Christian have to strengthen him against wrong conduct? _____ _____ (Matt. 7:7–11; Gal. 6:1–5)
5. What is the Christian's standard of conduct toward others? _____ _____ (Matt. 7:12)
6. In what areas of our lives do you feel we are most apt not to practice the Golden Rule? ____ _____

Study in small groups.—The general procedure in using small group study is to divide the class into two or more study groups with similar but different assignments. The number of groups is determined by the purpose of the study. For example, in studying the lesson, "How God Has Revealed Himself to Men" (John 1:1–14), there are three natural divisions of the passage. Three groups may be organized and assigned the task of outlining the ways in which God was revealed in: (1) John 1:1–5, (2) John 1:6–9, and (3) John 1:10–14.

After ample time for study has elapsed, the groups should be reconvened and reports given to the class. As the reports are given, they may be verified and discussed.

Build on assignments and reports.—Learning activities should not be confined to the lesson period and the classroom. In fact, learning is an ongoing process in which the learner must frequently gain a satisfying sense of completion. He must feel that he has created something for himself and by himself.

To help the learner enjoy the experience of fulfilling some purpose and solving some problem, the teacher should provide for inquiry and research through assignments.

A good assignment must be clearly stated, interesting to the learner, designed to stimulate thinking, and thoroughly integrated into the teaching plan.

In making assignments the teacher will need to indicate the sources of material, the form the assignment should take, and the amount of time to be used in reporting.

Assignments and reports should be used as naturally as possible in the lesson. They should not be labeled as "Assignment No. 1," and so on, but should be used as an integral part of the discussion. The teacher will need to alert each person participating by sharing a "lead" into the report.

When assignments are used in this way, many excellent teaching situations arise as the class members make their varying contributions and discuss the situations together.

Almost any lesson can be taught to advantage when it is built around the assigned activities of the members. For example, a lesson on salvation may be centered around several reports on what the "blank" denomination teaches about salvation. After the reports have been given, each doctrine should be substantiated or rejected by what the Scripture passages in the lesson teach.

Develop a logical or chronological outline.—Outline studies are overused to such an extent, and lend themselves so readily to "preaching" the lesson, that it may be unwise to consider their use. However, when used sparingly and wisely a logical or chronological outline is a good major study activity.

In studying the lesson, "God's Hand in History" (Isa. 10:5–15; 14:24–27), a logical outline may be used as the major Bible study activity. The points may be as follows:

1. God's punishing hand (Isa. 10:5–7)
2. God's judging hand (Isa. 10:12–15)
3. God's determining hand (Isa. 14:24–27)

It should be emphasized that the outline study should be used as a guide for discussion rather than as a talk. The use of questions, chalkboard, flip chart, and even assignments prevent the lesson from becoming a "tell-a-thon."

Spotlight special situations.—An excellent major study activity is to spotlight special situations such as contrasts, comparisons, characteristics, attitudes, conduct, and so on.

Using the lesson, "The Risen Life" (Col. 3:1–15), a study in contrasts may be used to spotlight the difference between the "old" life and the "new." As the class reads the lesson passage, a member may list on the chalkboard the characteristics of the two ways of life. The lists would appear as illustrated:

Old Life (Col. 3:5–9)	*New Life* (Col. 3:10–15)
1. Fornication	1. Mercy
2. Uncleanness	2. Kindness
3. Inordinate affection	3. Humility
4. Evil desire	4. Meekness
5. Covetousness	5. Longsuffering
6. Anger	6. Forbearance

7. Wrath
8. Malice
9. Blasphemy
10. Filthy talk
11. Lying

7. Forgiveness
8. Love
9. Peace

Dramatize an incident.—Many Sunday school lessons are drawn from exciting stories. Dramatizing these incidents makes not only an interesting Bible study activity, but it also allows for creativity and identification.

In the lesson, "I Believe God" (Acts 27–28), the class members may be given sheets of paper and asked to write a "Ship's Log" of Paul's journey to Rome as they read the passage. The result may appear as follows:

Ship's Log

Journey to Rome, fall of A.D. 58
1. Off for Rome (Acts 27:1)
2. Warning of danger (Acts 27:9–11)
3. Faith through a storm (Acts 27:14–26)
4. Witnessing on an island (Acts 27:44; 28:1,7–9)
5. A dream come true (Acts 28:16)

Use reviews and tests.—Reviewing a lesson should certainly be more than merely a rehash of old material. It should be a "new view," bringing fresh insights, interpretations, and more meaningful relationships.

The review should help the learner reorganize, appraise, and pass judgment on his learning progress. It needs to be emphasized that the purpose of the review is not only to discover how much the learner can recall but also to learn how much better he can think and bring his learning to bear on new problems and relationships.

Tests are generally considered as instruments of measurement; yet in the Sunday school they may serve even a better purpose as a major Bible study activity. There are many kinds of tests, and they are all useful for specific types of Bible study. The familiar knowledge test is useful in determining the present level of acquaintance with any given body of Bible content. The life situation essay, or "what-would-you-do" approach, is good for determining the learner's ability to bring Bible truth to bear on new situations.

The questionnaire may be used to determine a composite of class learning in any number of areas. The self-check test is one of the most popular ways of helping learners take a subjective look at themselves.

Several other interesting tests, such as conduct patterns, attitude scales, case studies, autobiographical records, and character growth tests may be used to facilitate objective Bible study.

One of the most practical ways to use a test as a major Bible study activity is to give the same test before and after a unit of study. The comparison of results on the two tests may be made at a monthly class meeting, thus creating an additional review opportunity. The following test illustrates the before and after technique. Members are asked to answer "true" or "false."

Personality Preview Test
(Correct answers are indicated.)

1. Mary was the "holy mother of God." (*F*)
2. Andrew was the classic example of a personal soul-winner. (*T*)
3. Matthew was a man of great prominence, loved by all, and highly respected as a citizen. (*F*)
4. Martha was especially devoted to Christ, while Mary was more practical and hospitable. (*F*)
5. Thomas denied the Lord and sold him for thirty pieces of silver. (*F*)
6. Dorcas was a wicked woman who loved to wear purple clothing. (*F*)
7. John Mark made a complete failure of his life and almost ruined Paul as well. (*F*)
8. Silas was a "hard-shell" who refused to support missions in the Jerusalem area. (*F*)
9. Timothy was a reckless young man given to "living it up." (*F*)
10. Lydia was a Gentile businesswoman who took advantage of Jewish proselytes. (*F*)
11. Titus was a competent young preacher who was completely trusted by Paul. (*T*)

12. Gaius was a layman in the Jerusalem church who loved the "spotlight." (*F*)

Use Additional Bible Study Activities in Supporting Roles

In addition to the major Bible study activity around which the lesson study is built, there should be other Bible searching opportunities. These additional passages of Scripture serve to support and undergird the major Bible study activity. Frequently the other references will be a part of the larger lesson, but any appropriate Bible material may be used in a supporting role.

Search for additional information.—Rarely ever does the major passage of Scripture being studied constitute the total Bible teaching on the subject. By using related selections, more details can be found, more information can be collected, and the truth being studied can be better highlighted.

A good Bible concordance and dictionary are excellent sources of help in searching for additional information about any particular truth. A good reference edition or teacher's Bible will also be useful in locating passages to study in a supporting role.

Verify a point of view.—Bible teaching worthy of the name frequently causes the members to reveal points of view that are not based on scriptural truth. When such a situation occurs, it offers the teacher a splendid opportunity to introduce an additional Bible searching activity, using the Bible in a supporting role.

There is a twofold value in introducing Bible-searching activities to correct unfounded points of view. This technique allows the teacher to clear up misunderstandings without making a frontal attack on the members. It also helps the members to develop the habit of going to the Bible to check out their ideas, concepts, and points of view.

Clarify hazy concepts.—Far too many class members have only a hazy concept of Bible truth. For example, even though they have a faint idea of many of the basic doctrines of their faith, they have difficulty in explaining or understanding the distinctive aspects of these teachings.

There is more truth than humor in the story that is told about the man who had just learned that Dan and Beer-sheba were towns instead of people. "I always thought they were husband and wife, like Sodom and Gomorrah," was his terse reply.

Teachers need to refrain from merely telling their members what is wrong when they are confused about Bible truth. Rather, they should make a practice of introducing Bible-searching activities that help the members clear up their own hazy concepts and confusion.

Study similar situations.—One of the best ways to use the Bible in a supporting role is to study another situation that is similar to the lesson. It is obvious, for example, that a lesson in one of the four Gospels can almost always be seen from two or more points of view.

The comparison of similar material gives additional details, different chronology, alternate objectives, and expanded or compounded truth.

Use passages that enrich meaning.—Perhaps the best way to use Scripture passages to support the main truth is to use material that enriches meaning. Few, if any, Bible truths appear in only one place in the Word. To introduce these appropriate passages of a supplementary, complementary, or contrasting nature is a mark of good teaching. Nothing reinforces truth more than having a larger measure of the truth introduced through enrichment material. In other words, the best way to illustrate, support, and enrich the lesson passage is to use additional passages of Scripture in supporting roles. Of course, there are certain limiting factors in using these additional passages. For example, (1) the major Bible study activity must not become submerged in a hodgepodge of reference running; (2) the aim of the lesson must be kept in view; and (3) the limited amount of time must be carefully budgeted.

8

The Laboratory of Life

Paul, in writing to Titus, says, "Tell men of these things, Titus. Urge them to action (2:15, Phillips).

"Please, teacher," said the little girl as she lingered after school, "tell me what I learned today. My daddy always wants to know."

Getting learning "back home" is always the difficult part of teaching, because learning has not really been achieved until lessons get into life. Teaching ends with the ringing of the bell, but real learning begins when the class adjourns.

The objective of a good Bible teacher is to make the truth of God's Word effective in the lives of those whom he teaches. Therefore, the lesson content must never be both the point to begin and the point to terminate learning. Lessons must become useful in life. It is essential that we understand that learning is for action, for use.

The Bible is a book of life. It came out of life to go back into life. The Bible is the way to life, the way of life, and the way into life. It is concerned with the whole of life.

These facts mean that Bible lessons must become personal and practical to the members, that Bible truth must be translated into useful learning, and that learning must be produced in the laboratory of living experience.

How Are Lessons Made Personal and Practical?

Two basic principles in teaching beg for consideration here. One is that learning is a personal matter. It is as individualized and unique as every member of the class. In a class of twenty members there will be twenty different ways of learning. These differences increase with experience and maturity.

A second principle to be considered is that of the teacher's role in learning. Although the teacher is many things, his foremost role is helper. He is a facilitator of learning. These two principles mean that the learner must do his own learning and that the teacher must help him to do so. This process of helping learners learn depends to a great extent on making Bible lessons personal and practical to the learner. There are at least three ways in which learning may be made personal.

Help the Learner Comprehend the Truth

As already implied, there must be a sharing of the responsibility for learning. There must be a creative search, both by the teacher and the learner, for meaning, understanding, and relevance. Even though comprehension may not come to a passive nonparticipative class member, the teacher bears much of the responsibility for making Bible truth crystal clear.

Illustrate the truth.—An appropriate illustration is the real power of teaching because it opens the windows of the mind. It is like "an angel writing in a book of gold."

An illustration must be closely related to the truth being discussed. It must be realistic and graphic enough for the members to identify themselves with it at once. Long, involved, and far-fetched illustrations that take longer to explain than to tell hurt rather than help learning.

Deepen the impression.—Comprehension is frequently thwarted because of weak, distorted, or wrong impressions. If truth is to be useful in life it must be understood clearly and comprehended fully. It must be clothed in deep impressions and trimmed in accurate concepts.

Deep impressions are made in several ways. For example, brief summaries, colorful repetitions, vivid recapitulations, and poignant reviews fix impressions accurately. Penetrating questions also deepen impressions and often stimulate the members to ask questions in return. Teachers may also deepen impressions by pointing out areas of a truth that have yet to be explored. This technique may stimulate learners to further study.

Involve the members in the search for meaningfulness.— Learning, to be complete, must involve the whole person. There must be thinking, feeling, acting on new insights, or learning simply does not result. Because of this fact, the learner must feel a compelling interest in the experience of learning. He must face his own doubts, perplexities, and problems before he develops a vital concern for coming to a knowledge of the truth.

To involve the members fully, the teacher must know and understand the learner. He must create situations which puzzle, irritate, bewilder, fascinate, or challenge the learner.

Some of these situations must be built into the teaching plan while some will arise in the give-and-take of the discussion.

Help the Learner Discover the Applications

Unapplied or unappropriated information is of little value, because the applications of truth are the important part of learning.

Plan a time for making applications.—Unfortunately, a teaching plan, because it is in writing, must indicate a definite place for "applications." It is illogical, however, to think that an individual learns passively and then, after learning, finds a way to apply his new knowledge. Actually, in the entire task of learning, there should always be some aspects of application being carried on. Nevertheless, there is a time in every lesson when it is appropriate to specifically apply truth to life, to make truth meaningful in the experiences of life.

Realize the necessity of self-activity.—Learning comes through self-activity, through the experience of thinking, feeling, and acting as a Christian. Therefore, learning that is significant is

self-appropriated. It comes as a result of investigation, exploration, and discovery. It follows, then, that class members should
not be told how a lesson applies to their life. They should be led
to discover the points of significance for themselves.

There are two great extremes in the life of the learner. On the
one hand, there is the way the learner thinks about a situation
and, on the other hand, how he feels about how he thinks. These
extremes must be reconciled if learning is to occur. It is the
learner's application of the truth that helps him correlate his
thinking and his feeling.

Lead the members through experiences of application.—To
lead the members through experiences of application the teacher
should (1) ask probing questions; (2) confront the class with
alternatives; (3) lead them into actual or imaginative predica-
ments that require application of the truth; (4) focus attention on
sub-Christian attitudes and activities; (5) allow the members to
express doubt, wonder, skepticism, and curiosity about points of
application; and (6) help the members interpret their own experiences.

What part does the teacher play in applying truth? He must
remember that one of the greatest problems in getting the members to apply truth is his excessive verbalism. Too much talking
causes the class members to accept the truth without applying the
truth. Time should be allowed for thinking, meditating, and
pondering. Generalizations and exhortations should be avoided.

How May Lessons Be Translated into Useful Learning?

One of the greatest concerns of Christian teachers is the great
gap between the things class members hear on Sunday and the
things they do on Monday. All too often teaching impressions are
not strong enough to stimulate living expressions of the truth. How
may this deficiency in teaching be overcome?

Relate the Truth to Daily Life

When a teacher neatly frames Bible truth in an outline and
holds it before a class for thirty minutes, making no vital connec-

tion with present life, he has missed the whole point of teaching. Jesus' teaching was remarkable in its concern for spiritual insight and action. All of his teachings were concerned with the daily life of his learners, and most of his teaching experiences began on a personal level.

It is, indeed, difficult to teach spiritual truth so that class members will have an accurate body of biblical truth, and at the same time know how to follow it. In order to achieve this ideal of using what one knows, it will be necessary for the teacher to organize "living experiences" with truth. Learners must be led to face life situations, problems that call for the use of Bible truth. Through actual or imaginary situations, the learner must see the principle at work in a hard, cynical, and materialistic world.

There is no sure way to guarantee a high level carry-over of lessons into life, but the following activities may be considered basic and essential.

Stimulate mental participation.—The cognitive processes— thinking, meditating, and judging—are essential to real learning. If lessons become learning, members must be led to think about the meaning of the lesson to themselves, and to others. Learners should recall past experiences that are related; they should make a reflective or deliberative choice.

Elicit emotional response.—In the areas of attitudes, appreciations, ideals, and interests all learning is strongly emotionalized. Emotional responses, when properly controlled and directed, are extremely important in turning lessons into useful learning. It is quite necessary, therefore, that learners feel properly if they are to achieve a spirit of reverence, develop a wholesome attitude, gain a new appreciation or ideal, find a balanced sense of values, express a Christian conviction, or deal with a personal shortcoming.

Solicit a personal action.—Lessons are actually reproduced in life when members are led to practice a new truth or insight in daily life. For example, members may begin a definite plan of witnessing, undertake a specific Bible study program, visit a denominational institution, or render a definite service.

Diagnose Spiritual Deficiencies

Lessons must touch life at the point of spiritual deficiency. Only as learners face their own weaknesses and shortcomings do they make learning a part of themselves and put it into actual practice.

Caution and great care should be exercised by teachers in dealing with the spiritual problems of the members. Frontal attacks, exhortations, or crusades are rarely ever in order. An indirect approach is much more fruitful. It is better to (1) spotlight a sub-Christian attitude; (2) pinpoint a wrong spirit; (3) probe an improper feeling; (4) rethink a prejudiced opinion; or (5) analyze a spiritual problem.

In effect, the members must be led to see themselves, not only as others see them, but as they are mirrored in the light of God's Word.

Stimulate the Learners to Respond

Both Christian teaching and learning are finally the work of the Holy Spirit. It is, therefore, an awesome responsibility to work in harmony with the Spirit and not seek to achieve one's own desires in the life of the learner. Teachers should not take advantage of a learner or coerce him into an insincere response. On the other hand, members do not actually learn until they make an appropriate response to truth.

Jesus did not always achieve immediate results, but every one of his contacts led his pupils one step closer to abundant life. Teachers, too, should patiently work for a response that is appropriate to each member. They should pray for and work toward the time when their members will make Christian choices and decisions. The teacher should strive for a response that will engage the learner in Christian action.

When class members respond appropriately to the lesson, the Holy Spirit, and the teacher, they are able to put the truth to work. Then lessons become useful learning, and the quality of Christian character and conduct is enhanced.

How Is Learning Projected into Life?

There is an ancient maxim that says, "Practice makes perfect." Although this statement is generally accepted as a sound educational principle, it is also true that the practice of error creates a habit pattern of error.

It is evident that Jesus used the practice principle in his teaching. He sent out the twelve, and later the seventy, to practice the art of visitation. He sent the woman at the well back to town to give her testimony.

Secular educators know the value of the doing phase of learning. The young doctor diagnoses and practices under instructors; the law student argues cases in "mock court"; the new schoolteacher practices under supervision—all to get their learning into life.

The process of getting lessons into life is generally called projection. The devices used are known as carry-over activities. Projection, or carry-over, is achieved when class members practice Christian traits, virtues, and skills until they habitually respond and react in a Christian manner. It is in this way that learning is projected into life.

Although some educators think that a carry-over activity is not essential to every lesson, it seems that every lesson ought to have one if "practice makes perfect."

Select Carry-over Activities Democratically

Ideally, in learning, the learners themselves should plan an activity that will allow them to put the principle of the lesson into daily use. Practically, however, most classes will need the guidance of their teacher in the selection and implementation of carry-over activities. Even in helping, however, the teacher should elicit the activity, not hand it out.

Certainly the carry-over should grow out of the personal interests and spiritual needs of the class members. It should come as a concensus agreement and provide for personal participation even if it is a group activity.

Find an Activity That Is Appropriate

To be an appropriate activity, the carry-over should grow naturally out of the major or central truth of the lesson. It should be related to the aim of the lesson and the unit. It should be conducive to habits of permanent value. Therefore, something to be done daily is preferred. In some cases, especially when changed conduct is sought, the carry-over could be continued throughout the group unit.

The carry-over activity should be simple and not too time-consuming, since it ought to be done each day during the week.

Time Carefully the Use of Carry-over Activities

There is probably always a "best" time to bring the carry-over activity into the picture. The time will be determined by several factors, such as the age of the members, the type of lesson material, the readiness of the class, and the type of expected activity.

Waiting until the end of the lesson period to introduce the activity is not at all necessary. Carry-over activities may be introduced and developed in at least four "time zones": (1) the activity may develop as the lesson text is interpreted; (2) the activity may be brought in incidentally as a part of the lesson discussion; (3) the activity may come out at the climax of the lesson; or (4) the activity may arise as a deliberate part of a summary or review of the lesson.

Evaluate the Carry-over Experiences

Reporting on and evaluating the experiences of the members has several learning values: (1) the "gentle persuasion" of reports encourages the members to participate in the activity; (2) reports and evaluations help the teacher verify the accuracy of the learning experiences; (3) the reports offer an abundance of unplanned opportunities for additional teaching; and (4) report sessions stimulate the members to help each other as they develop Christian character.

Reports and evaluations should not be allowed to consume a great deal of time on Sunday morning. Actually, some of the reports could be used at the monthly class meetings.

Class members of all ages are essentially curious. They like to explore, investigate, and discover. Carry-over activities, therefore, have great appeal. Interests impel learners to learn, but their interests must be organized and guided into productive channels before lessons really get into life.

9

Stimulating Lesson Study

Because Sunday school attendance is a voluntary matter, it is assumed that most of the members come with at least some desire to learn. It is not uncommon, however, for teachers to face the fact that many members need encouragement, if not strong stimulation, to study the lesson before they attend the class session. All too frequently it is necessary to spend so much time on Sunday morning in getting the basic facts of the Bible passage before the members that there is little time for anything else.

Bible material should be mastered at home through advanced study of the lesson so that the teaching period can be used for learning in depth, for meeting the spiritual needs of the members.

It is not easy to get advance preparation. However, the patient, conscientious teacher may be able to secure a high degree of lesson study by using the following suggestions.

Consider the Reasons for Failure to Study

In teaching, just as in medicine, diagnosis is an essential prelude to success. To learn why members do not study is basic to discovering ways to whet their appetite for study. Teachers should not be "taken in" by the shopworn excuse "too busy." This excuse is so thinly veneered that it is not acceptable. People always find time for the things they really want to do.

Why is preliminary study frequently lacking? Are there any valid reasons why class members do not prepare the lesson?

Lesson preparation is not expected.—Is it unrealistic and too old-fashioned to expect class members to prepare the lesson before attending Sunday school? Honesty demands an immediate admission that many members do not prepare or even read the Bible passage in advance of the class period. Is this failure an indication that they will not prepare, or is it evidence that they have not been expected to prepare? Actually, there is an element of truth in both ideas. The major difficulty, however, is that members have been conditioned to look upon the teacher as a bearer of predigested Bible truths, which the members are expected to absorb. The members have been led to believe that learning is simply listening politely to the teacher's stockpile of Bible knowledge. In other words, they have actually been trained or conditioned not to study.

Some teachers do not expect their members to do advanced study because it does not fit into their concept of teaching. These teachers view teaching as "bringing the lesson." They seem to feel that teaching is pouring material into empty vessels. Teachers who have this static view of teaching do not really want the members to prepare the lesson. Members who prepare are always wanting to ask questions, discuss a point, or share an experience. These activities upset the teacher who has prepared a straight lecture on the lesson. It is necessary for the "telling" teacher to have unprepared members to assure their own equanimity.

Lesson study is not made essential.—The teacher who monopolizes the class session causes advance study on the part of the members to be unimportant, if not completely unnecessary. What incentive to advanced preparation could possibly endure when the members know that the teacher plans to rehearse the entire lesson? Under such circumstances it is unfair to blame class members entirely if they fail to study.

The teacher must accept his share of the responsibility for getting members to prepare the lesson. He must teach in such a way that a knowledge of the lesson is essential. Then the members will take time to prepare.

The satisfaction of learning is absent.—It is only as the learner feels a sense of satisfaction and becomes aware of his spiritual progress that he is challenged to make worthy preparation for the class session. Therefore, the wise teacher will plan to teach in such a way that the members (1) find new ideas, (2) experience new reactions, (3) gain spiritual illumination, (4) develop broader appreciations, (5) find deeper understandings, (6) grow in strength of will, and (7) make Christian decisions.

In these experiences there will be ample satisfaction in Bible study and adequate motivation for advanced preparation. In this way learning becomes a personal, dynamic experience of growth, which brings an abiding satisfaction to the learner.

Lessons seem unrelated.—When lessons are taught as isolated, minute sections of truth, there is no apparent relationship to each other. This kind of teaching reduces Bible truth to abstract generalities with little or no application to life. Learning comes by associating old ideas and experiences with new ideas and experiences. Learning comes by relating the known to the unknown, by making lessons relate to each other, by connecting the parts with the whole.

Helping class members understand the relationship between lessons, units, and objectives is one of the teacher's best tools in getting lessons studied in advance.

Bible truth is not applied to life.—Learning of any kind, even the learning of Bible truth, is greatly hindered if there is no apparent application to life and to life needs. The older the class members the more significant is this fact, because learners become much more selective as they mature. As the learners become more conscious of the great amount of learning that is needed, the more they are inclined to pass over that which has no apparent application to their personal needs.

Teachers who assume their responsibility for helping learners find the relevance and usefulness of Bible truth are taking the first step toward getting prepared lessons.

Until learners find life-related applications of the Word of God, they are learning the Bible simply as words. To be sure these are inspired words, but they become the "living Word" only as they are incorporated into the heart, thoughts, and mind of the learner.

Just as interest is the key to learning, application is the major force behind lesson preparation.

Help the Members to Learn How to Study the Lesson

In his lesson preparation, the sincere member of a Bible class desires something more than a mere cursory reading of the Bible passage and lesson comments. He wants to study in a logical and enjoyable fashion. When he learns how to do this, he may participate intelligently in the discussion and development of the lesson on Sunday morning.

Reading the lesson.—The key to understanding anything is the reading and rereading of the various accounts. Someone has said, "We do not know the Bible because we do not read the Bible." In the preparation of the Sunday school lesson it is very essential that the member carefully and prayerfully read the printed portion of the lesson text.

It would also be helpful to read the same passage in two or more modern speech translations of the Bible. At this particular time in lesson preparation, it would be well to read the larger Bible lesson.

After the reading of the lesson text in the various translations and versions of the Bible, it is well to read the lesson comments in the pupil's quarterly. As the reading progresses the learner should underline the main truths as he sees them revealed in the pages of the quarterly. Anything that is not understood should also be underlined. After the detailed reading of the lesson itself, it is well to reread the printed portion of the lesson text.

Studying the details.—Although a careful reading of the text is important, this is not enough for a complete understanding of the lesson. The details of the lesson must be understood as well. Perhaps the most logical place to begin is to look up the pronunciation of unfamiliar words. Following the use of the dictionary, it is well to discover the explanation and meaning of the various figures of speech. This procedure enables the class member to know whether the incident being studied is a historical event, a parable, a metaphor, hyperbole, or some other mode of expressing a Bible truth.

In studying the details of the lesson it is important to discover the authorship of the book, the setting of the book, and the purpose for which the passage was written. This information can be gained by consulting a good reference Bible, Bible dictionary, concordance, commentary, or other lesson helps such as *Broadman Comments*.

To conclude the studying of the details, it would be good for the learner to prepare a brief outline of the lesson passage. This outline would not be concerned with the comments in the quarterlies but simply three or four points which set forth the heart of the Bible passage itself.

Thinking about the meaning.—As a class member prepares the Sunday school lesson, it is important that he review the lesson titles for the quarter. Each lesson is a part of a unit which generally covers an entire quarter. Each of the lessons has a specific relationship to all of the others. Therefore, the study of the lesson should include a thorough thinking through of the relationship of the lesson being studied to the previous lessons in the quarter.

While thinking about the meaning of the lesson, it is most helpful to jot down the central truth of the lesson. As a rule, the central truth of the lesson is not revealed as such, but it is always very apparent in the lesson treatment. Learning to identify the central truth is a very important part of study.

Thinking about the meaning of the lesson would also include a time of meditation on the meaning of the lesson to the individual. Lesson preparation is not as much a mental preparation as it is a personal preparation. To discover what the lesson has to say to the individual personally is actually the heart of lesson preparation.

Evaluating the results.—Evaluation is generally thought to be the highest level of learning. It is, therefore, essential that the learner develop some skill in evaluating the results of his study. A valuable type of evaluation is to analyze any personal questions or problems related to the lesson which come to mind. This analysis should be followed by a consideration of any course or courses of action that the lesson suggests. Evaluation would also include listing any unresolved questions about the lesson which the learner would like to bring up in the class session.

Summarizing the study.—The final step in lesson preparation is to summarize the results of the study. This may be done by reviewing the truths that have been underlined in the quarterly and the Bible. Summarizing the study would call for a frank, honest appraisal of the individual's life in the light of the lesson which he has studied.

In the event the teacher has made any personal or group assignments, these assignments should now be prepared.

Use Teaching Procedures That Require Advance Study

Study, like learning, must be motivated and energized. To be of maximum value, motivation should be intrinsic, that is, generated within the learner himself. Actually, the teacher cannot motivate a learner; the learner must motivate himself. However, the teacher may help the learner want to study. Eventually in one way or the other, the learner must be helped to want to study.

The records, personal recognition, and promotional plans help motivate the learner with an external "push." This type of motivation is called extrinsic motivation.

To stimulate real and abiding motivation, the teacher must learn how to build bridges between the lesson material and the interests, needs, and problems of the learner. Furthermore, the teacher must learn to do this bridge building so expertly that the learner eventually learns to do the bridge building himself.

It is imperative that the teacher become proficient in providing strong incentives for study. The use of a teaching plan, as proposed in this book, plus the use of the various techniques which have been discussed, constitute the major activity of the teacher in providing strong incentives for study. It will become apparent to the alert teacher that the same devices or activities that arouse interest in the lesson at the beginning of a session may also be used to stimulate interest in the following lesson. In general, these activities are those which arouse the curiosity of the learner, and curiosity is the key to interest.

The concern of this chapter has been the stimulation of the class members to prepare the lesson before attending the class session. As a final step of the teaching plan, let us consider *stimulating study of the next lesson.*

As a rule, not more than two or three minutes will be required to achieve this purpose. The teacher should not be tempted to overlook this final step of the teaching plan simply because the time required is brief. In fact, this period is so important that these two or three minutes will greatly determine what happens in the thirty minutes of the following Sunday session. How then may the teacher arouse the class members' interest and give them a purpose for study?

Use a question and a related comment.—The question is probably the most useful teaching device known. Possibly, one would be an excellent teacher if he learned to master the question and its use.

To illustrate the question and related comment activity, let us suppose that there is a lesson on Titus. The procedure would be somewhat as follows:

Question: Would you name your son "Titus"? If your name (or your husband's name) were Titus, would you want a nickname?

Comment: Next Sunday's lesson is about a man who bore the name of Titus, and who by his character and life gave the name significance. As you study the lesson, see whether your feeling about the name changes to any degree. As you study, write down any change of feeling as it occurs.

Use an object and related statement.—Visual motivation is always useful in stimulating lesson preparation. An actual object, a picture, a projected picture, a drawing, a chart, a graph, a poster, a flip chart, or other visual materials may be suitable. Assume that next Sunday's lesson is a study of Silas. The procedure for stimulating study could be somewhat as follows:

Object: Display a can of food from which the label has been torn so as to disguise its contents. Say, "This can contains food for the body." Hold up the Bible and say, "This book contains food for thought. Many churches are filled with willing workers. A few are willing to do all the work—others are willing to let them. As you study the lesson for next Sunday, think about the category into which Silas falls. Make a list of the reasons that support your conclusion."

Use a statement to be verified or rejected.—The chalkboard is the teacher's partner in teaching. It should be used as often as possible. It is especially useful in stimulating study for the next lesson. As an illustration, think of a lesson on Thomas. Perhaps the title would be, "Thomas: Through Doubt to Faith."

Statement: Write on the chalkboard, "He who has never doubted has never really believed." Ask, "Is this statement true or false? Let your lesson study help you reach a decision."

Relate an illustration and follow with questions.—Stories, illustrations, and personal experiences are excellent devices for stimulating study. In a lesson on the power of the tongue, an illustration with related questions is most appropriate.

Illustration: Say, "Last week I went to the doctor for a physical checkup. The first thing he asked me to do was to stick out my tongue."

Questions: Ask, "Have you had this experience? James, the writer of the book that bears his name, would say that there are far more important reasons than physical for 'sticking out the tongue.' Can you discover what these reasons are? In your lesson preparation for next week make a list of these reasons as you discover them."

Stimulate verbal responses to a word on the chalkboard.—A device used by psychologists is called the word association test. This same device is useful in stimulating lesson preparation. If the lesson were to be "Christ Gives Life Eternal," the following word association might be used.

Word: Write on the chalkboard the word "death."

Verbal response: Ask the class for their first thought on seeing the word death. Ask whether their feeling about death corresponds to the scriptural teachings. Suggest that before the members prepare the lesson they jot down their feelings about death. After a study of the lesson, jot down what the Scriptures teach. Compare the before and after lists.

Use study guides.—A study guide is a very useful instrument in both personal and group learning. Teachers should spend time, if necessary, in learning how to perfect this tool. They should also involve the members in the preparation of study guides. For a lesson titled, "Who is Jesus?" the following use of a study guide would be helpful.

Study guide: "Please look at the four questions which have been written on this study guide sheet which we have distributed. See whether you can discover the answers to these questions as you study next Sunday's lesson. Write brief answers to the questions along with Scripture references and bring the study guide to class next Sunday. The study guide will be the basis for our lesson discussion."

Use Scripture searching for a particular statement or word.— The best Bible study is always purposeful Bible study. That is, one learns most when he is searching for something specific. In one of the frequent evangelistic lessons, perhaps on the subject, "You Must be Born Again," a search for a particular statement or word would be an appropriate motivation.

Search: Say, "In the Scripture passage for next Sunday's lesson, Jesus made a very startling statement to Nicodemus. The statement is unusually significant, and it has a very personal meaning for every person alive. Search for that statement in your own Bible as you study next week's lesson. Try to formulate in your own words a statement of what Jesus meant when he made the unusual disclosure to Nicodemus."

Use assignments and reports.—The teacher who feels that

class members, even older members, are not interested in assignments and reports, either does not understand poeple or has not tried these devices recently.

In one of the series of studies on either the major or minor prophets of the Old Testament, a lesson title might be "False Leadership Brings Ruin." The use of an assignment would be very appropriate for this type of lesson.

Assignment: Say, "In the lesson for next Sunday another prophet comes on the scene. When you have studied about him, write a brief headline about him that could have appeared in the local paper. Bring the headline with you when you come next Sunday. We will begin the lesson by comparing headlines."

The teacher must look upon himself and his class members as partners in learning. Within this framework the teacher has a threefold function: (1) to create a favorable condition for learning; (2) to help the members face problems and reach decisions in the light of the Scriptures; (3) to provide a sustained challenge through learning. The study of the members and their personal preparation for the class session are extremely important to the teacher. Teachers may use the preparation as a threat, a duty, or a challenge. Those who see the study of the members as a challenge are far more likely to arrive at the ideal of "partners in learning."

TEACHING PLAN SHEET

I. ESTABLISHING THE DIRECTION OF THE LESSON

Date: _____

Unit Title: _____

Unit Aim: _____

_____

_____

Lesson Title: _____

Lesson Passage: _____

Central Truth of Lesson (a simple statement that reflects the heart of the lesson passage and pinpoints the idea in the lesson title): _____

_____

_____

_____

Life Needs of the Members (a brief list of spiritual needs toward which this lesson can be directed): _____

_____

_____

_____

Lesson Aim (a concise statement of the learning outcomes toward which the teacher will direct the learning activities and experiences of the members):

_____

_____

_____

_____

_____

_____

II. GUIDING THE LEARNING ACTIVITIES OF THE MEMBERS

STEP 1: Creating a Readiness for Learning (1-3 minutes)

Use a device that is (1) centered in life (2) interesting enough to catch attention immediately (3) slanted to call for member response (4) suitable to lead directly into Bible study.

STEP 2: Making Bible Study Purposeful (10-15 minutes)

Use activities that (1) give the members something to discover or a problem to solve (2) involve the members in actual Bible study (3) survey the entire passage (4) isolate important verses for special study (5) locate the central truth (6) reveal new insights.

(continued next page)

_____

_____

_____

_____

_____

_____

_____

_____

_____

_____

_____

_____

_____

_____

_____

_____

_____

STEP 3: Getting Bible Truth into Life (10-15 minutes)

Use activities (1) that relate the applications to the aim (2) that are true to the Bible teaching (3) that are geared to getting members' suggestions (4) that are within the realm of members' interests, abilities, and needs (5) that commit the members to action (6) that secure a definite carry-over activity.

_____

_____

_____

_____

_____

(continued next page)

_____

_____

_____

_____

_____

_____

_____

_____

_____

_____

_____

_____

_____

_____

_____

STEP 4: Stimulating Study of Next Lesson (1 minute)

Use an activity that (1) arouses the members' curiosity (2) gives them a purpose for study.

_____

_____

_____

_____

_____

_____

_____